NZ RUGBY STARS
COOKBOOK

NZ RUGBY STARS
COOKBOOK
COOKING FROM THE HEART

Photography by Tamara West and Kieran Scott

ALL ROYALTIES TO THE NEW ZEALAND RUGBY FOUNDATION

ALLEN&UNWIN
SYDNEY•MELBOURNE•AUCKLAND•LONDON

RUGBY FOUNDATION

CONTENTS

INTRODUCTION & ACKNOWLEDGEMENTS

Welcome to the New Zealand Rugby Foundation's second foray into publishing. We would like to acknowledge the enthusiasm and professionalism of Allen & Unwin in guiding us through the process.

The Rugby Foundation was formed in December 1986, the brainchild of the great All Black Kel Tremain and Hawke's Bay philanthropist Sir Russell Pettigrew. Both have now passed away, leaving a legacy the entire New Zealand rugby family is very proud of.

Things have moved on significantly since then, with our core business now focusing on partnering with our VIPs—Very Injured Players—financially and emotionally. We raise funds to enable us to support the work we do, partnering with New Zealand Rugby (NZR) and ACC (Accident Compensation Corporation) to communicate the message of safety first. The excellent RugbySmart programme, jointly developed by NZR and ACC, is a leader in world rugby.

We are a national organisation, partnering with 97 VIPs. For the most part our VIPs have suffered SCI (Spinal Cord Injury) or TBI (Traumatic Brain Injury), with the majority of them living in wheelchairs, but they are certainly not defined by this. They have families and loved ones whose lives were also changed in a heartbeat, and we are here to support them too. Among those we work with, the longest-standing injury was sustained in 1966 and the most recent occurred in 2017.

Our income streams are diverse. The Rugby Foundation operates under a policy of not dissipating its accumulated funds. Future-proofing of the organisation is vital, as we know that VIP numbers increase by about one per annum. We rely heavily on gaming trusts, fundraising events and our generous sponsors and donors, including both organisations and individuals. We receive great support from New Zealand Rugby, who provide us with an annual grant.

This publication will add another string to our bow.

We know too well that people only engage with us when they 'need to'. It is terribly confronting to suddenly be caught up in the trauma of catastrophic injury. The foundation is the first line of assistance, focusing on 'instant support' and later, as players rehabilitate, on bridging the gap between the 'before' and 'after' quality of life for both the players and their families.

For us at the foundation, particularly me and our Commercial Manager, Ben Sturmfels, working on this book has been a labour of love. We would like to acknowledge all the people who contributed recipes; the step-up from everyone has been heart-warming. Ben and I were blown away by the support we received from those who gave up their time to appear in the photo shoots—we are hugely grateful to them. Extra-special thanks to Kieran Read and Wyatt Crockett for gracing the front cover. Cheers, guys!

Thank you to New Zealand Rugby for their blessing, especially Todd Barberel and Nick Smith, and Rachael Spencer for the individual player biographies.

Our grateful thanks to the NZRPA (New Zealand Rugby Players' Association) for so effectively activating your networks. Thanks also to the franchise management teams and coaches who accommodated our photo shoots in between busy training schedules. Huge thanks to NZRPA Personal Development Managers Victoria Hood (Blues), Lloyd Elisara (Chiefs), Arden Perrot-David (Hurricanes), Virginia Le Bas (Crusaders) and Mark Ranby (Highlanders).

Some big magic wands were at play to make schedules work.

The shoots took place in a number of franchise bases and at Blake Park in Tauranga, as well as in private homes—our grateful thanks to Phil Booth, Neil Cudby, Keith Jarvie and Dane Coles. The Kelliher Estate also played a vital role, with Grahame Dawson and his team opening the doors to the magnificent homestead and gardens on Puketutu Island.

On behalf of us all at the foundation, grateful thanks to Kieran Scott and Tam West for their beautiful photography; Kathy Paterson for her incredible talents in testing and cooking the food for the photo shoots; and Jenny Hellen and Leanne McGregor from Allen & Unwin.

Finally, heartfelt thanks to our readers. Enjoy the book—tell your friends, buy a second one! It is the unwavering support from rugby lovers and food lovers like you that makes such a difference to this excellent cause.

Lisa Kingi-Bon
Chief Executive Officer
New Zealand Rugby Foundation

Contributors pictured in frontmatter and chapter openers: page 2: Israel Dagg & Seta Tamanivalu; page 4: (clockwise from left) Fiao'o Faamausili, Graham Mourie, Tane Norton, Nehe Milner-Skudder, Niall Williams & Tyla Nathan-Wong; page 8: Matt Duffie & Akira Ioane; page 9: Nathan Harris, Damian McKenzie & Keenan Alexander; page 44: Nathan Harris; page 45: Ben Smith; page 76: Damian McKenzie; page 77: Sam Cane; page 102: Kieran Read & Wyatt Crockett; page 103: Rieko & Akira Ioane; page 138: Kelly Brazier, Sarah Goss & Ruby Tui; page 139: Robbie Hewitt & Keenan Alexander; page 156: Dane Coles & Bob Symon; page 157: Dane Coles.

LIGHT MEALS

CHUNKY SMOKED SEAFOOD CHOWDER

SERVES 4

25 g butter
1 small leek, trimmed and finely
   sliced
2 medium-sized potatoes, cut
   into 2-cm pieces
500 ml chicken or vegetable
   stock
1 bay leaf
1 stick celery, trimmed of strings
   with a vegetable peeler and
   finely sliced
1 cup frozen corn kernels
400 ml full-cream milk
salt and freshly ground white
   pepper
200 g deboned smoked fish,
   flaked
8 smoked mussels, coarsely
   chopped
small handful of flat-leaf parsley
   leaves, finely chopped

TO SERVE

1 lemon, cut into wedges
crusty bread

Place the butter in a heavy-based saucepan and melt over a low heat. Add the leek and cook until soft but not coloured.

Add the potato pieces, stock and bay leaf. Bring to a gentle boil, cover the pan, lower the heat and simmer until the potato pieces are soft, 15–20 minutes.

Add the celery, corn and milk, bring back to the boil and simmer gently, uncovered, for a further 10 minutes. Season with salt and pepper.

Remove and discard the bay leaf, then add the smoked fish and mussels to the pan. Gently stir in the chopped parsley.

Serve the chowder in warmed soup bowls with lemon wedges for squeezing and slices of crusty bread alongside.

MATT DUFFIE debuted as an All Blacks outside back in 2017 during the Vista Northern Tour against the Barbarians. Matt plays for North Harbour in the Mitre 10 Cup and the Blues in Investec Super Rugby. In 2011 Matt played one Test for the Kiwis rugby league side against Australia.

CHICKEN AND CORN SOUP

SERVES 4

1 store-bought whole cooked chicken
1 litre good-quality chicken stock
1 tablespoon light soy sauce
1 teaspoon finely grated fresh ginger
1 cup frozen corn kernels
4 spring onions, trimmed and finely sliced
1 stick celery, trimmed of strings with a vegetable peeler and finely sliced
200 g egg noodles, cooked according to packet instructions and drained
2 eggs
juice of ½ lemon

Remove the chicken meat from the whole chicken, shred it and set it aside.

Pour the chicken stock into a large saucepan and add the soy sauce, ginger and corn. Place over a medium heat and cook, stirring occasionally, for about 5 minutes.

Add the spring onion and celery and cook for a further 2–3 minutes until the celery is tender.

Drop in the noodles and chicken, and stir gently for a few minutes to heat the chicken through. Taste for seasoning, adjusting with a few extra drops of soy sauce if necessary. Remove from the heat.

To thicken, whisk the eggs and lemon juice together until frothy. Add a ladleful of hot stock from the soup to the egg mixture and whisk in. Tip this mixture into the soup and stir to mix.

To serve, lift the noodles out first and divide them between warmed bowls, then ladle in the soup.

TANE NORTON is a former All Blacks captain who first won selection for the national side in 1971 against the British and Irish Lions. He also played for the New Zealand Māori side and was awarded the Tom French Memorial Cup for the outstanding Māori Player of the Year in both 1973 and 1974. Tane was President of New Zealand Rugby in 2003. He has been on the Rugby Foundation board since 1999, and was President from 2014 to 2017. He has also been the rangatira representative in Christchurch and has spent countless hours at the Burwood Spinal Unit with players and their families.

DAMIAN MCKENZIE
MUSSEL FRITTERS

SERVES 4

¼ cup white wine

2 kg live mussels in the shell, scrubbed and de-bearded

1 shallot, very finely chopped

finely grated zest of 1 lemon

3 tablespoons finely chopped flat-leaf parsley

1 tablespoon torn basil leaves

3 eggs, separated

½ cup standard flour

½ teaspoon baking powder

1 tablespoon milk

sea salt and freshly ground black pepper

oil for shallow-frying

TO SERVE

bread and butter

1 lemon, cut into wedges

Heat the wine in a large saucepan over a medium-high heat. Add half the mussels and cook for a few minutes, until they just open. Remove to a bowl, and cook the remaining mussels the same way. Discard any that do not open.

Strain the mussels, reserving the cooking liquid. Remove the mussels from their shells, discarding the brown tongues. Set aside to cool.

Place half the mussels in a food processor and pulse until finely chopped. Transfer to a bowl. Finely dice the remaining mussels by hand. Place in the bowl with the processed mussels, then add the shallot, lemon zest and herbs.

Lightly whisk together the egg yolks and 2 tablespoons of the reserved cooking liquid. Add to the mussel mixture and stir to combine.

Sift the flour and baking powder together, then stir into the mussel mixture along with the milk and salt and pepper. Beat the egg whites until soft peaks form when you lift the beater up. Fold a tablespoonful of egg white into the mussel mixture to loosen it, then carefully fold in the remaining egg white.

Coat the base of a frying pan with oil and heat **over a medium-high heat** until the oil is hot. Drop tablespoons of the mussel mixture into the pan and cook for 2 minutes on each side, until golden and cooked in the centre. Repeat with the remaining mixture.

Serve with slices of buttered bread and lemon wedges.

TIP

• *Also delicious with your favourite tomato chilli chutney and a green salad.*

Invercargill-born **DAMIAN MCKENZIE** debuted for the All Blacks in 2016. He also plays as fullback for the Chiefs Super Rugby club, and has represented New Zealand with the Māori All Blacks and the New Zealand Schools and U20s teams.

SOY CHICKEN NIBBLES

SERVES 6

1 kg chicken nibbles or chicken wings
1 tablespoon vegetable oil
2 cloves garlic, finely chopped
¼ cup dark soy sauce
2–4 tablespoons sugar, to your taste

Preheat the oven to 180°C. Line a shallow baking tray with foil and baking paper (this helps with the washing up). Place the chicken nibbles or wings in the baking tray in a single layer.

Place the oil and garlic in a small frying pan and place over a low heat. Warm until gently sizzling, then cook, stirring, for 30 seconds. Remove from the heat and stir in the soy sauce and sugar. Pour the mixture over the chicken and place in the oven. Bake for 35–40 minutes, until the chicken is cooked through and a lovely rich, golden colour.

I like to serve this with steamed white rice and steamed or pan-fried bok choy.

TIP

- *My grandfather cooks the chicken on top of the stove in a large pan over a medium heat, stirring continuously until the chicken is cooked.*

TYLA NATHAN-WONG was the youngest player ever to be selected for the Black Ferns Sevens team when she made her debut as an 18-year-old in 2012. She was a key member of the team that lifted the Sevens World Cup a year later. Tyla captained the team during the 2017 season and is in the top five all-time point scorers in the World Series.

Clockwise from top left: Fiao'o Faamausili; Tyla Nathan-Wong; Tane Norton; Sir Bryan Williams.
Opposite: Graham Mourie & Tyla.

ISRAEL DAGG

SALMON TERIYAKI & COLESLAW SLIDERS

SERVES 4

TERIYAKI SAUCE

1–2 tablespoons white sesame
  seeds
1 tablespoon sesame oil
1 clove garlic, crushed
2.5-cm piece of fresh ginger,
  peeled and very finely grated
2 tablespoons soft brown sugar
5 tablespoons light soy sauce
5 tablespoons mirin
1 teaspoon cornflour
4 tablespoons cold water

COLESLAW

4 handfuls of finely shredded
  green cabbage
1 handful of finely shredded red
  cabbage
1 carrot, peeled and coarsely
  grated or finely shredded
1 spring onion, trimmed and
  finely sliced
2–3 tablespoons mayonnaise
1 tablespoon olive oil
1 tablespoon apple cider vinegar
salt and freshly ground pepper

SALMON

500 g piece of fresh salmon,
  bones removed
juice of 1 lemon
flaky sea salt

TO SERVE

8 slider buns, split and toasted if
  desired

Preheat the oven to 180°C.

Place a small, dry frying pan over a medium heat. When hot, add the sesame seeds and toast for a few minutes until lightly golden and fragrant, shaking the pan frequently to prevent the seeds burning. Tip onto a plate and set aside to cool.

Place the sesame oil in a small saucepan over a medium heat. Add the garlic and ginger and cook gently for a few minutes until aromatic. Add the brown sugar and stir, then add the soy sauce and mirin and stir in. Reduce the heat to low and simmer, uncovered, for about 3 minutes.

In a cup, mix together the cornflour and water to make a slurry and stir into the sauce. Add the sesame seeds and simmer, uncovered, for a further 5 minutes, stirring occasionally to prevent the sauce sticking. Set aside.

Place the cabbage, carrot and spring onion in a bowl. In another bowl, combine the mayonnaise, oil and vinegar. Stir through the cabbage mixture, taste for seasoning and adjust with salt and pepper. Set aside to allow the flavours to mingle.

Line a shallow baking tray with baking paper, leaving a good overhang as you are going to wrap the salmon in this paper. Place the salmon in the middle of the paper, squeeze over the juice of the lemon and sprinkle with a little flaky salt.

Cover the salmon with paper, twisting the edges together so you have a sealed package. If you have difficulty sealing it properly, cover the tray in foil as well. Bake for about 20 minutes or until the salmon is cooked to your liking.

Remove from the oven, carefully open up the paper and pour the teriyaki sauce over. Leave to cool for about 10 minutes.

To serve, fill the buns with coleslaw and pieces of teriyaki salmon.

ISRAEL DAGG was first selected for Hawke's Bay when he was a teenager at secondary school. Following his Test debut for the All Blacks in 2010, he became a regular for the All Blacks and was part of the successful 2011 Rugby World Cup side. Israel has the second-most starts at fullback on the All Blacks all-time list.

EGGPLANT STACK

SERVES 4

1–2 eggplants (depending on size—you need 8 slices)

olive oil, for brushing

4 rashers rindless streaky bacon, diced

250 g button mushrooms, wiped clean and sliced

salt and freshly ground black pepper

4 tablespoons pesto

2–3 large ripe tomatoes, sliced

125 g tub cherry buffalo mozzarella, or 1 large buffalo mozzarella, sliced (optional)

a few basil leaves

balsamic vinegar, for drizzling

Heat a char grill or barbecue grill until hot. Preheat the oven to 180°C. Line a shallow baking tray with baking paper.

Slice the eggplant lengthwise into 8 even-sized slices. In batches, brush the slices with olive oil and place on the hot grill. Grill for 3–5 minutes on each side until dark grill lines appear and the eggplant flesh is soft. Transfer each batch to a plate when cooked.

Heat a frying pan over a medium heat and add the diced bacon. Cook, stirring occasionally, until lightly golden, then add the sliced mushrooms. Cook until the mushrooms begin to soften. Season with salt and pepper.

Lay out 4 grilled eggplant slices on the prepared tray. Smear each with a tablespoon of pesto, then layer with tomato slices and the bacon–mushroom mixture. If desired, add the buffalo mozzarella and a few basil leaves. Top each with the remaining eggplant slices. Place in the oven to warm through for about 15 minutes.

When ready, remove from the oven and serve drizzled with a little balsamic vinegar and a few extra basil leaves. If you like, serve with a simple leafy green salad dressed in a lemon vinaigrette.

ROSS ORMSBY was injured in a scrum while playing 1st XV rugby in Te Awamutu in 1984, when he was 16. He became a tetraplegic, and because he couldn't work on the family farm he did a business degree at university. This led him into small business, not-for-profit work and roles on boards. Ross has contributed to many clubs and was awarded life membership to Waikato University Netball.

TIPS

- *It is no longer necessary to salt eggplant slices before cooking, as a lot of the bitterness has been bred out of today's eggplants.*
- *Eggplants should not have seeds that are very hard or too pronounced; if so, they are overmature.*
- *For a vegetarian alternative, replace the bacon with sundried tomatoes and chopped black olives. You could also swap out the mozzarella for cottage cheese or sliced Brie or Camembert. Use your favourite chutney to add more flavour.*

MUSHROOM, HERB & CHEESE OMELETTE

SERVES 1

3 large eggs
salt and freshly ground black
   pepper
1 tablespoon chopped parsley
   and chives
2 good knobs of butter
handful of sliced button
   mushrooms
½ cup grated melting cheese,
   such as Gruyère

Break the eggs into a bowl. Season with salt and pepper, and add the herbs. Mix well using a fork.

Heat a small non-stick frying pan over a medium heat. Add a good knob of butter, then add the mushrooms. Cook until the mushrooms begin to colour, about 5 minutes, then transfer to a plate.

Add the remaining knob of butter to the pan and allow to melt. When the butter is sizzling, add the eggs. Leave to cook until the eggs are almost set but still a bit liquid on top.

Sprinkle in the cooked mushrooms and then the cheese. Remove the pan from the heat. Loosen the edge of the omelette from the pan with a small spatula. Fold over one side of the omelette to enclose most of the filling, then slide it onto a warmed plate and serve straight away.

BRODIE RETALLICK has cemented his status as a world-class lock thanks to his high work rate and uncompromising attitude, as well as his confidence in performing the lock's core role. He made his debut for the Chiefs Super Rugby side and his debut for the All Blacks just a few months apart in 2012.

BRAD SHIELDS

HOMEMADE PIZZA

MAKES 2 LARGE PIZZAS

DOUGH

¾ cup warm water
1 teaspoon active dry yeast
2 cups high-grade or bread flour,
  plus a little extra for sprinkling
1½ teaspoons salt

TOPPING

2 cups thick tomato purée
1 large firm but ripe avocado,
  halved, stone removed, peeled
  and sliced
2 cups grated mozzarella
8 slices prosciutto
soft goat's cheese, for spreading
¼ cup toasted pumpkin seeds
freshly ground black pepper
a few olives, preferably with
  stones removed

TIP

• *To toast the pumpkin seeds,
  heat a small, dry frying pan
  over a medium heat. Add the
  seeds and cook for 1–2 minutes,
  shaking the pan until they pop
  and begin to colour. Transfer to
  a plate to cool.*

Pour the water into the warmed bowl of an electric mixer fitted with a dough hook. Sprinkle the yeast over the water and leave for 5 minutes until the yeast begins to froth. If the yeast doesn't froth within this time, your water may not be warm enough (start again if this happens).

Sift in the flour and salt. On low speed, knead the dough until it is smooth, shiny and no longer sticky. If the dough is too sticky you may need to add a little more flour, but avoid this if possible.

Place the dough in a lightly oiled bowl, cover with plastic wrap and a clean tea towel and leave to rise in a warm place until the dough has doubled in size, about 1 hour in warm weather.

Preheat the oven to 230–240°C. Place an oven rack in the bottom third of the oven and place a heavy baking tray on the rack to preheat.

Divide the dough in half. On a lightly floured bench, roll and pat one piece into a large oval or round. Remove the tray from the oven, dust it with a little flour and place the dough on top. Working quickly, spread with half the tomato purée and top with half the avocado slices and half the grated mozzarella. Bake until the crust is golden and the cheese is melted. The cooking time will depend on the heat of your oven and how thick or thin you rolled the dough.

Remove from the oven and transfer the pizza to a board. Top with prosciutto slices. Smear a little goat's cheese on each prosciutto slice and grind over some pepper. Sprinkle with olives and pumpkin seeds.

Repeat with remaining dough and topping ingredients. Cut into slices and serve.

BRAD SHIELDS is a much-loved Wellington rugby player who captained the Hurricanes Super Rugby side to an outstanding come-from-behind draw against the British and Irish Lions in 2017. Brad also represented New Zealand in the U20s team that won the 2011 IRB Junior World Championship.

Clockwise from top left: Dane Coles; Muir Templeton; Brad Shields making a variation on his homemade pizza; Dane & Brad. Opposite: Brad Shields.

BLUEBERRY SMOOTHIE

MAKES 1

½–1 cup fresh or frozen
  blueberries
1 ripe banana, peeled
1 teaspoon runny honey or
  1 pitted Medjool date
2 cups chilled coconut water
handful of ice cubes

Place the blueberries, banana, honey or date, coconut water and ice in a blender and whizz to combine. Pour into a glass to serve.

TIP
• *I use 1 scoop of vanilla protein powder in my smoothie instead of the banana.*

SETA TAMANIVALU debuted for the All Blacks in 2016 off the back of powerful campaigns for the Chiefs and Crusaders in Investec Super Rugby. He plays for Taranaki in the Mitre 10 Cup and was New Zealand's provincial player of the year at the start of his career in 2014.

OKA I'A (FISH SALAD)

SERVES 4

500 g boneless and skinless
  snapper or trevally, cut into
  1-cm dice
¼ cup lemon or lime juice
¼ red onion
2 medium-sized ripe tomatoes
2 small cucumbers (Lebanese
  cucumbers are good here)
2 spring onions, trimmed
1 cup coconut milk
sea salt

Place the diced fish in a ceramic or glass (non-reactive) bowl and pour over the lemon or lime juice. Stir, then set aside while you prepare the vegetables.

Chop the onion, tomatoes and cucumber into small dice. Finely slice the spring onions.

Drain the fish and discard the juice. Add the red onion, tomato and cucumber to the fish. Pour the coconut milk over the fish, season with salt and gently mix to combine. Cover and place in the fridge for 30 minutes to allow the flavours to mingle.

Serve well chilled.

TIPS

- *Only use the freshest fish available when making Oka I'a.*
- *If you like, add a little finely chopped chilli and coriander leaves to the fish salad.*

NAFI LEFONO was injured playing club rugby in Dunedin on 31 March 2007. There were tough times transitioning to the idea of life in a wheelchair, but Nafi finished his physiotherapy degree in 2014 and now works as a Wheelchair and Seating Therapist. He has played for the Wheel Blacks over a number of years, made some great mates and travelled all over the globe. Family is very important to him, and his parents and siblings have supported him on this journey.

AHI TUNA POKE

SERVES 4

900 g very fresh raw tuna loin,
  cut into bite-sized chunks
½ sweet white onion or red onion,
  finely diced
2–3 spring onions, trimmed and
  sliced
2 teaspoons white sesame seeds
4 tablespoons light soy sauce
1½ tablespoons sesame oil
2 teaspoons grated ginger
about 2 teaspoons brown sugar
flaky salt (optional)

Combine all the ingredients except the sugar and flaky salt in a bowl and gently mix to coat the tuna. Taste and add just enough sugar to offset the soy sauce. You can also add a pinch of flaky salt or more sesame oil or soy sauce if desired.

Place the poke in the fridge to marinate for at least a few hours before serving.

I like to serve it with some slices of fresh coconut and a few drops of Samoan chilli sauce for a bit of a bite.

TIPS
- *Poke (pronounced poh-kay) is a popular Hawaiian dish. The word simply means 'cut into chunks'.*
- *While poke is traditionally made using raw ahi (yellowfin or bigeye) tuna or cured octopus, you could try another medium to firm fish, such as fresh kahawai or trevally. The key is to use very fresh fish. You can also make a more substantial meal of it by serving it 'bowl style' over steamed rice and with various chopped vegetables and condiments.*

SIR MICHAEL JONES was elected to the New Zealand Rugby Board in April 2018. The former All Black played 74 matches between 1987 and 1998 and is a member of the World Rugby Hall of Fame. He was knighted in 2017 for his work in driving economic and social development for Pasifika people in New Zealand and the Pacific region, and holds the Samoan matai chief titles of Savae and Laauli.

Clockwise from top left: Tane Norton; Graham Mourie; Sir Bryan Williams & Graham; Sir Bryan.

JOHN (TERRY) WRIGHT

POMELO & PRAWN SALAD

SERVES 4

DRESSING

2 cloves garlic, crushed

1 red chilli, de-seeded and finely chopped

1 teaspoon finely grated fresh ginger

juice of 1 lemon

1 tablespoon fish sauce

1 teaspoon brown sugar, or more to taste

SALAD

2 thin slices fresh ginger

1 stalk lemongrass, light green part only, bruised

1 spring onion, trimmed and sliced

pinch of salt

500 g raw prawn cutlets

1 large pomelo or grapefruit or 3 oranges

2 medium carrots, peeled

small handful of mint leaves

small handful of coriander leaves

TO SERVE

cos lettuce or radicchio leaves, torn if large

a few fried shallots

handful of roasted and roughly chopped peanuts

Place all the dressing ingredients in a bowl and whisk to combine. Set aside.

Place the ginger slices, lemongrass, spring onion and salt in a saucepan with the prawn cutlets. Add enough cold water to just cover, and place over a low heat. Bring to a gentle simmer and cook, uncovered, until the prawns have just turned pink. Drain and refresh under cold water to stop the prawns cooking. Spread out on paper towels to drain and cool completely. If the prawns are large, you can chop them roughly if you like.

If using a pomelo, you can peel the fruit and segment it by hand, doing your best to remove the outer pith. To get a tidy result with grapefruit or oranges, use a sharp knife. Slice off the top and bottom of each piece of fruit and place the fruit on a board, cut side down. Starting at the top and using downward strokes that follow the contour of the fruit, slice the skin away from the flesh, leaving no white pith. Cut the fruit into segments by slicing along the membranes.

Slice the carrots lengthwise and shred them into long strips. Place the prepared fruit, carrot and herbs in a large bowl. Add the cooled prawns and toss gently to combine. Drizzle in the dressing and gently toss again.

To serve, place the cos leaves on a large plate and fill each with the prawn salad. Top with a few fried shallots and a sprinkling of peanuts. Extra coriander leaves are great here, too.

JOHN (TERRY) WRIGHT played 34 matches for the All Blacks between 1986 and 1991. He made 135 appearances for Auckland, scoring 112 tries, and in Ranfurly Shield rugby he finished with an incredible 53 tries in 52 matches. Terry was also a regular member of national sevens sides, appearing in 11 major tournaments.

BROCCOLI & BACON SALAD

SERVES 4

DRESSING

¼ cup good-quality mayonnaise
1 tablespoon apple cider vinegar
1 teaspoon grainy mustard
salt and freshly ground black or
  white pepper

SALAD

1 small head broccoli, cut into
  small florets
4 rashers rindless streaky bacon
1 small red onion, very finely
  sliced
2 handfuls of cherry tomatoes,
  halved horizontally
2 teaspoons toasted white
  sesame seeds
2 teaspoons toasted pumpkin
  seeds
finely grated zest of ½ lemon
  (optional)

TO SERVE

crusty bread (optional)
creamy goat's cheese

In a small bowl, mix together the mayonnaise, vinegar and mustard. Season with salt and pepper. Transfer to a small serving bowl, cover and keep in the fridge until needed.

Preheat the oven grill until hot.

Steam the broccoli until bite-tender. You can test the broccoli stalks with the point of a small sharp knife—the knife should slip through easily. Place the steamed broccoli in a shallow serving bowl.

Place the bacon rashers under the hot grill, and grill until crispy on both sides, turning once. Remove the bacon and place on paper towel to drain.

Add the red onion and cherry tomatoes to the broccoli and sprinkle with the toasted seeds and lemon zest, if using. Crumble the grilled bacon over the top.

Serve the salad with crusty bread slices spread with creamy goat's cheese, or crumble the cheese over the salad. Serve the dressing on the side for people to help themselves.

TIP

• *To toast the white sesame seeds, heat a small, dry frying pan over a medium heat. Add the seeds and cook until they begin to colour and you can smell them toasting. Transfer to a plate straight away to prevent over-toasting. Add the pumpkin seeds to the pan and cook for 1–2 minutes, shaking the pan until they pop and begin to colour. Transfer to a plate to cool.*

Now in his early forties, **DION SEELING** was 18 when he was injured playing rugby for Tauranga Sports in the Bay of Plenty. He had just been selected to trial for the national under-19 team and dreamed of a professional rugby career. That dream ended on 5 July 1995, when the talented young flanker fell awkwardly during a match and broke his neck. Dion now runs a clothing and design business with his wife, Merle, and works as an artist from his studio at home.

LIMA SOPOAGA

ROASTED BUTTERNUT PUMPKIN, SAUSAGE & PEARL BARLEY

SERVES 4

½ cup pearl barley, rinsed

600 g butternut pumpkin, peeled and cut into 2.5-cm cubes

3 tablespoons olive oil

salt and freshly ground black pepper

1 tablespoon sweet marjoram leaves, chopped

1 tablespoon white wine vinegar

4 sausages (fresh chorizo are good here, or pork sausages)

¼ cup toasted pumpkin seeds

small handful of coriander leaves

DRESSING

1 teaspoon bittersweet smoked paprika

2 tablespoons lemon juice

5 tablespoons extra virgin olive oil

Wellington-born **LIMA SOPOAGA** was a member of the New Zealand U20s side that won the Junior World Championship in 2015, and he debuted for the All Blacks later that year. In 2018, after playing 16 Test matches for the All Blacks, Lima signed a two-year deal with English Premiership side Wasps.

Preheat the oven to 190°C. Line a shallow roasting tray with baking paper.

Bring a saucepan of lightly salted water to the boil. Add the pearl barley and boil gently for 30 minutes, until tender. Drain and set aside to keep warm.

Place the butternut cubes in a bowl, pour 2 tablespoons olive oil over them and season with salt and pepper. Stir through the sweet marjoram. Tip the butternut out onto the prepared tray and spread out in a single layer. Sprinkle over the vinegar. Place in the oven to roast for 25–30 minutes, until tender, turning the butternut cubes halfway through cooking.

Heat the remaining 1 tablespoon olive oil in a large frying pan over a medium heat. Add the sausages and cook gently, turning occasionally, for about 20 minutes until cooked through and well browned. Remove from the pan and set aside to keep warm.

In a large bowl, whisk together the dressing ingredients. Add the warm pearl barley and stir to mix well. Add the roasted butternut pumpkin.

Slice the sausages on the diagonal into thick slices and add to the bowl. Stir gently to combine, then place in a shallow serving bowl. Top with the pumpkin seeds and coriander.

TIP

• To toast the pumpkin seeds, heat a small, dry frying pan over a medium heat. Add the seeds and cook for 1–2 minutes, shaking the pan until they pop and begin to colour. Transfer to a plate to cool.

Clockwise from top left: Ruby Tui; Kelly Brazier; Dion Seeling; Sarah Goss.
Opposite: Kelly & Sarah.

SEAFOOD
& POULTRY

PAN-FRIED CRISPY SALMON WITH WATERMELON SALAD

SERVES 4

WATERMELON SALAD

1 kg watermelon, cut into thick slices

2 good handfuls of cherry tomatoes, halved horizontally

½ telegraph cucumber, cut into pieces or slices

4 small radishes, cut into wedges

1 small red onion, very finely sliced

juice of 1 small lemon or lime

2 tablespoons extra virgin olive oil

salt and freshly ground black pepper

2 tablespoons toasted pumpkin seeds

small handful of mint leaves, shredded

SALMON

4 thick salmon pieces (125–150 g each), skin on, bones removed

oil, for rubbing

flaky salt

TO SERVE

1 lemon, cut into wedges

leafy green salad (optional)

Remove the skin from the watermelon slices and cut each slice into smaller pieces. Place these in a shallow serving bowl as you go. Add the cherry tomatoes, cucumber, radish and red onion. Squeeze the juice of the lemon or lime over the top and drizzle with oil. Season with salt and pepper, then sprinkle with the pumpkin seeds and mint.

Heat a large frying pan over a high heat. Rub the salmon skin with a little oil and flaky salt. Place in the hot pan, skin side down, and pan-fry until the skin is crispy, 1–2 minutes. Reduce the heat to medium-high, turn the salmon over and pan-fry the flesh side for 3–4 minutes. The salmon will cook a little further once removed from the pan so it is better to be slightly under rather than over.

Serve the crispy salmon with lemon wedges for squeezing over, and the watermelon salad alongside. Add a salad of green leaves too, if you wish.

TIP

• *To toast the pumpkin seeds, heat a small, dry frying pan over a medium heat. Add the seeds and cook for 1–2 minutes, shaking the pan until they pop and begin to colour. Transfer to a plate to cool.*

Defensive rock **OFA TUUNGAFASI** debuted for the All Blacks in 2016. He also represented New Zealand at age-grade level and played two seasons with the New Zealand Schools side. The big prop plays for the Blues in Investec Super Rugby and for Auckland in the Mitre 10 Cup.

GOSS'S HERB & FENNEL BAKED FISH

SERVES 4

1 kg whole snapper, cleaned and scaled

2 lemons

sea salt

good handful of mixed fresh herbs (thyme, oregano, sweet marjoram, flat-leaf parsley)

1 small onion, thinly sliced

1 small fennel bulb, very thinly sliced

3 cloves garlic, roughly chopped

1 tablespoon olive oil

Preheat the oven to 220°C. Line a large, shallow baking tray with foil and baking paper, leaving a good overhang on all sides (you will use the overhang to wrap the fish).

Place the snapper on a board and score the skin horizontally on both sides, going halfway through the flesh and along the length of the spine. Score on an angle across the back of the head. Place the snapper in the lined tray.

Halve one lemon and squeeze the juice over the snapper and inside the cavity. Season with salt. Slice the remaining lemon. In a bowl, combine the sliced lemon, herbs, onion, fennel and garlic. Tuck this mixture into the cavity and drizzle the snapper with the olive oil.

Cover the snapper with the baking paper and foil, rolling the edges together to seal the parcel. Bake for 25–30 minutes.

Remove the snapper from the oven and open up the parcel. Spoon the cooking juices over the snapper a few times.

I like to serve this fish with a green herb dressing or a salsa (make your own salsa by chopping up ripe tomatoes, red or spring onion and a little chilli). A simple leafy green salad lightly dressed with lemon vinaigrette would be great, too.

TIP
- *Open up the parcel for the last minutes of cooking to colour the snapper a little.*

GRAHAM (GOSS) MOURIE is a former All Blacks captain and former coach at the Hurricanes Super Rugby club. Graham, whose international debut was in 1977 in the successful match against the British and Irish Lions, famously removed himself from selection for the controversial 1981 Springboks Tour. Later that year Graham was made a Member of the Order of the British Empire for services to rugby. Graham has been on the Rugby Foundation board since 2016.

SIMPLE FAMILY FISH PIE WITH A PASTRY LID

SERVES 4

500 ml full-cream milk

1 slice of onion

1 bay leaf

3 parsley stalks (reserve leaves for another use)

a few whole black peppercorns

50 g butter, plus extra for greasing the dish

3 tablespoons standard flour, plus extra for rolling pastry

600 g firm white fish fillets, skinned and boned, cut into 2.5- to 3-cm pieces

finely grated zest of 1 lemon

2 tablespoons finely chopped parsley

salt and freshly ground pepper

300 g flaky puff pastry

1 egg, lightly beaten (egg wash)

TO SERVE

1 lemon, cut into wedges

SONNY BILL WILLIAMS has been a national and international champion across rugby, rugby league and boxing. Sonny was a member of the 2011 and 2015 Rugby World Cup-winning All Blacks sides and he also joined the New Zealand Sevens team for the Rio Olympics.

Preheat the oven to 200°C. Lightly grease a 4-cup-capacity pie dish. Place a pie bird or an upturned ovenproof egg cup in the centre of the dish if you have one.

Pour the milk into a heavy-based saucepan and add the onion slice, bay leaf, parsley stalks and peppercorns. Place over a low heat and let the milk come slowly up to simmering point. Remove from the heat and set aside for 5 minutes to allow the flavours to infuse. Strain into a jug, discarding the solids. Rinse out the saucepan.

Place the butter in the saucepan and melt over a low heat. Increase the heat to medium. Sift in the flour and stir to make a roux, cooking and stirring until lightly golden. Pour the infused milk into the saucepan and stir continuously until the sauce is smooth, shiny and thick enough to coat the back of a wooden spoon. Gently stir through the fish, lemon zest and chopped parsley. Season with salt and pepper and transfer to the pie dish.

On a lightly floured bench top, roll out the pastry until 5 mm thick and large enough to cover the top of the pie dish, with a little extra left over. Cut thin strips from the remaining pastry and place them around the edge of the pie dish. Brush with some egg wash.

Place the pastry lid on top of the filled pie dish and press the edges together. Using a sharp knife, make short horizontal cuts along the edges of the pastry. This is called 'knocking up' and it helps the pastry form layers that will puff up during baking. Make 2–3 slits in the middle of the pastry top to allow steam to escape during cooking (if not using a pie bird) and brush with remaining egg wash.

Bake for 25–30 minutes, until the pastry is golden and the filling is bubbling. Serve with lemon wedges for squeezing over.

Clockwise from top left: Akira Ioane; Ofa Tuungafasi; Nafi Lefono; Dan Buckingham.
Opposite: Sonny Bill Williams & Patrick Tuipulotu.

DAN BUCKINGHAM

PAELLA

SERVES 4

250 g boneless and skinless
  chicken thighs
200 g chorizo
12 mussels
6 large raw prawns
1 red onion
1 red capsicum
2 zucchini
4-5 cloves garlic
5 cups chicken stock
pinch of saffron threads
6 tablespoons olive oil
1½ cups paella (medium-grain)
  rice
400 g can chopped tomatoes,
  drained
zest of 2 lemons

TO SERVE

1 lemon, cut into wedges
good handful of flat-leaf parsley
  leaves, chopped

DAN BUCKINGHAM broke his
neck playing club rugby in 1999.
His injury focused his energies
and he was a Wheel Black for
16 years, then took up wheelchair
track racing, breaking the New
Zealand half marathon record in
2018. He is the general manager
of a TV production company,
as well as being chair of The
Attitude Trust and deputy chair
of the Disability Advisory Panel
for Auckland Council. He lives in
Auckland with his girlfriend, Sam.

Cut the chicken thighs into 2.5-cm pieces and the chorizo into
1-cm slices, keeping the meats separate. Scrub the mussel
shells clean, remove the beards and set aside. Shell and clean
the prawns and set aside.

Cut the onion and capsicum into 2.5-cm pieces and transfer
to a bowl. Slice the zucchini and add it to the bowl. Finely chop
the garlic, keeping it separate.

Pour the chicken stock into a saucepan, add the saffron and
place over a medium heat. Bring up to the boil, then reduce
the heat to low and keep the stock hot.

Place the oil in a paella pan or large, heavy-based frying pan
and heat over a medium-high heat. When the oil is hot, add
the chicken pieces and brown on both sides. Add the chorizo
and brown on both sides.

Reduce the heat to medium and add the onion, capsicum and
zucchini. Cook, stirring gently from time to time, for 2 minutes.

Add the prawns, mussels and garlic, and cook, stirring gently
from time to time, until the prawns turn pink and the mussels
open. Transfer the prawns and mussels to a plate and set the
plate aside.

Add the rice to the pan and stir to coat the grains with oil.
Pour in the saffron-infused chicken stock, together with the
tomatoes, and bring the mixture up to the boil. Reduce the
heat to low and simmer gently, uncovered, for 20 minutes
until the rice is just cooked.

Just before the end of the cooking time, add the lemon zest
to the pan and return the prawns and mussels to the paella.
Remove the pan from the heat, cover with foil and leave to
stand in a warm place for 10 minutes.

Serve the paella sprinkled with parsley and topped with
wedges of lemon.

SIR BRYAN WILLIAMS

CHICKEN 'N' COCONUT

SERVES 4–5

½ cup standard flour
1 large egg, beaten with 2
  tablespoons water
1½ cups dried white breadcrumbs
1 kg chicken drumsticks (about
  10 small drumsticks)
6 tablespoons vegetable oil
2 medium-sized onions, finely
  sliced
400 ml can coconut cream
salt and freshly ground black
  pepper

TO SERVE
1 lemon, cut into wedges

TIP
• *Coconut cream tends to
  separate in the can, so shake it
  well before opening.*

Preheat the oven to 190°C.

Place the flour on a plate, the beaten egg mixture in a shallow bowl, and the breadcrumbs on another plate.

In turn, coat each chicken drumstick in flour, shaking off excess, then dip in the egg mixture. Place in the breadcrumbs, turning and pressing the breadcrumbs on to make sure each drumstick is evenly coated. Set aside on a large plate.

Heat 2 tablespoons of oil in a large frying pan over a low heat. Add the sliced onion and cook gently, stirring occasionally, for about 5 minutes or until soft. Place in an ovenproof dish with a well-fitting lid.

Increase the heat to medium. Add 2 more tablespoons of oil and, once the oil is hot, add half the chicken drumsticks and brown them on all sides. Transfer them to the ovenproof dish in a single layer. Repeat with the remaining oil and drumsticks.

Pour the coconut cream around the chicken drumsticks. Season with salt and pepper, cover and place in the oven. Bake for 40 minutes, then remove the lid and bake for a further 15–20 minutes until the chicken is cooked through.

Serve hot with lemon wedges for squeezing over the chicken drumsticks. A big bowl of steamed green vegetables would go nicely alongside.

SIR BRYAN WILLIAMS played for the All Blacks 113 times, including 38 Tests between 1970 and 1978. After retiring from playing, Bryan coached club sides Ponsonby and Auckland, going on to become an assistant coach with the Hurricanes in Investec Super Rugby. His incredible commitment to rugby saw him knighted on the New Year Honours list in 2018. He has been on the Rugby Foundation board since 2014.

TERIYAKI CHICKEN

SERVES 4

2 tablespoons soft brown sugar
5 tablespoons mirin
5 tablespoons cooking sake
5 tablespoons light soy sauce
6–8 small chicken thighs,
   boneless and skinless
3 tablespoons standard flour
   (optional)
2–3 tablespoons vegetable oil

TO SERVE

white sesame seeds, toasted
steamed rice
Israel Dagg's coleslaw (see
   page 20)

In a small saucepan, combine the sugar, mirin, cooking sake and soy sauce. Place over a medium heat and bring to a gentle boil. Immediately reduce the heat and simmer, uncovered, for 1–2 minutes. Set aside.

Place the chicken thighs on a chopping board. Using a sharp knife, lightly score both sides of each thigh in a criss-cross pattern. Cover with plastic wrap or baking paper and use a meat mallet, the end of a rolling pin or the base of a small, heavy saucepan to pound the chicken until flattened. Dust with the flour, if desired (this prevents the chicken sticking to the pan).

Heat the oil in a large frying pan over a medium-high heat. In batches, add the chicken and cook for 2–3 minutes on one side, then turn and cook the other side for a further 2–3 minutes or until cooked through.

Add enough sauce to the pan to lightly coat the chicken, and cook until lightly caramelised. (Any extra sauce can be kept in the fridge for another time; it will keep for about 2 weeks.)

Serve chicken thighs on top of steamed rice with some coleslaw on the side. Sprinkle with toasted sesame seeds.

TIP

- *To toast the sesame seeds, heat a small, dry frying pan over a medium heat. Add the seeds and cook until they begin to colour and you can smell them toasting. Transfer to a plate straight away to prevent over-toasting.*

Current All Blacks captain **KIERAN READ** made his debut in 2008 against Scotland. His 19 consecutive wins as All Blacks captain from 2012 to 2016 is a world record. Kieran became the All Blacks' seventh Test centurion in the third Test against the British and Irish Lions in 2017.

FIAO'O (FI) FAAMAUSILI
CHOP SUEY

SERVES 4

500 g chicken thighs, boneless and skinless

dash of dark soy sauce, plus extra to taste

250 g vermicelli

3 tablespoons vegetable oil (peanut oil is good too)

1 small onion, diced

4 cloves garlic, very finely chopped

5-cm piece fresh ginger, peeled and very finely grated

OPTIONAL VEGETABLES—
CHOOSE FROM:

1 good handful broccoli pieces, steamed

1 good handful green beans, trimmed and steamed

1 red pepper, very finely sliced

1 carrot, peeled, sliced and steamed until just tender

1 good handful snow peas, trimmed and steamed

2–3 baby bok choy, cut in half and steamed

Cut the chicken into even-sized dice (about 2.5 cm) and place in a bowl with a dash of soy sauce. Mix to coat the chicken in the sauce, and set aside.

Place the vermicelli in a large heatproof bowl and add just-boiled water until just covered. Leave to soak until translucent, following the packet instructions. Drain, reserving ½ cup of the soaking liquid. Toss 1 tablespoon of vegetable oil through the vermicelli to prevent it sticking.

Heat another 1 tablespoon of vegetable oil in a large, wide saucepan or deep frying pan over a low heat. Add the onion and cook, stirring occasionally, until soft, 5–7 minutes. Add the garlic and ginger and cook, stirring, for a further 1 minute. Transfer to a bowl.

Increase the heat to medium, add the remaining vegetable oil and place the chicken in the pan. Fry the chicken, turning it to brown on all sides, until cooked through, about 10 minutes. Cut a piece open to check whether it is cooked—it should be pale all the way through, with no pink showing.

Add the onion mixture to the pan with the chicken and stir through. If you wish, add some steamed vegetables as well. Add the vermicelli and the reserved soaking liquid, and heat through, stirring gently. Season with extra soy sauce and serve immediately.

TIPS

• *Ensure that you don't over-soak the vermicelli, otherwise it will become very sticky.*

• *If you prefer, use light soy sauce rather than dark.*

Regarded as one of the world's leading hookers and most successful captains, **FIAO'O (FI) FAAMAUSILI** has been an integral part of the Auckland Storm provincial side, with over 90 appearances. Fi has captained the Black Ferns since 2012 and led the side to their Women's Rugby World Cup title in 2017—her fifth World Cup campaign.

Clockwise from top left: Sione Molia & Kurt Baker; Neil Cudby; Kurt & Sione; Sione & Sam Dickson.
Opposite: Kurt, Sione & Ross Ormsby.

CAJUN CHICKEN THIGHS

SERVES 4

POTATO WEDGES (OPTIONAL)

4 large floury potatoes, peeled
  (Agria potatoes work well)
2 tablespoons olive oil
salt and freshly ground black
  pepper, or use a dried garlic and
  herb seasoning powder

CHICKEN THIGHS

4-6 chicken thighs, boneless and
  skinless
oil, for rubbing
4 teaspoons Cajun seasoning
  powder

TO SERVE

1 ripe avocado, halved, stone
  removed and peeled
juice of ½ lemon
salt and freshly ground black
  pepper
4 soft corn tortillas, warmed
  following the packet instructions
4 handfuls of shredded lettuce
2 large ripe tomatoes, diced small
½ telegraph cucumber, diced
  small
1 small red onion, very thinly
  sliced
4 tablespoons mayonnaise
bittersweet smoked paprika, for
  sprinkling
2 teaspoons thyme leaves, for
  sprinkling

If making the potato wedges, preheat the oven to 200°C. Line a shallow baking tray with baking paper.

Cut the potatoes into large wedges and place in a bowl. Drizzle the oil over them and season to taste. Toss well to coat the potatoes in oil, then tip out onto the tray and spread out in a single layer.

Place in the oven to cook for 40–45 minutes, until golden, crispy and cooked through.

Heat a large frying pan over a medium-high heat. Rub the chicken with a little oil, then with the seasoning powder. Place in the hot pan and cook for 8–10 minutes, turning to brown on both sides. Cut the thickest thigh in half to check that it is completely cooked through. When done, remove the chicken from the pan and cover it with foil to keep it warm.

Mash the avocado and season with lemon juice, salt and pepper. Spread onto the corn tortillas, then top with the lettuce, tomato, cucumber and red onion.

Cut the chicken into strips and divide between the tortillas. Drizzle with mayonnaise and sprinkle with a little smoked paprika and thyme. Serve with the potato wedges on the side, if desired.

TIP

- *During summer when fresh sweetcorn is at its peak, add grilled corn to the salad. Remove the husks and silks from a cob of corn and grill on a hot barbecue grill for 10-12 minutes, turning frequently. Use a sharp knife to run down each side of the corn cob to remove the kernels.*

SAM DICKSON represented New Zealand in Aussie Rules before switching focus to rugby sevens. He made his debut for the All Blacks Sevens in Dubai in 2012 and is now an established member of the team. Sam's strength and agility, alongside his relentless defence, make him a key player for the side.

PAUL WILLIAMS

CHICKEN TIKKA MASALA

SERVES 4

2 tablespoons vegetable oil

1 onion, finely chopped

2 cloves garlic, crushed

2 teaspoons finely grated fresh ginger

1 tablespoon smoked paprika (I like to use bittersweet smoked paprika)

1 tablespoon ground cumin

2 teaspoons garam masala

1 teaspoon ground turmeric

¼–½ teaspoon dried red chilli flakes

500–600 g chicken thighs, boneless and skinless, cut into 2.5-cm pieces

400 g can chopped tomatoes in juice

finely grated zest and juice of 1 small lemon

½ teaspoon salt

125 ml cream

salt and freshly ground pepper

TO SERVE

cooked spinach or rainbow chard leaves

cauliflower rice

good handful of coriander leaves

Heat the oil in a deep, heavy-based frying pan (one with a lid) over a low heat. Add the onion and cook, stirring occasionally, until the onion is soft and beginning to colour, 5–7 minutes. Add the garlic and ginger and cook, stirring, for a further 30 seconds. Add the spices and cook, stirring, for a few minutes until aromatic, ensuring that they don't burn.

Add the chicken pieces and stir to coat the chicken in the spices. Stir in the tomatoes, lemon zest and juice, salt and cream. Cover the pan and simmer for 10 minutes, until the chicken is cooked through and the sauce has thickened. Taste for seasoning and adjust with salt and pepper.

Serve with cooked spinach or rainbow chard and cauliflower rice, topped with coriander leaves.

TIPS

- If you would like to add a little spice and sweetness to your Chicken Tikka Masala, stir in 1 tablespoon of sweet chilli sauce before serving.
- To make cauliflower rice, place ½ head of cauliflower florets in a food processor and pulse until the texture resembles that of rice or couscous. Heat in the microwave on high for 1–2 minutes or heat in a frying pan with a little butter. Season with salt and pepper before serving.

Professional referee **PAUL WILLIAMS** has extensive experience in New Zealand provincial rugby and made his Investec Super Rugby debut in 2016. His Test debut came in 2017 when he oversaw the match between Ireland and Fiji in Dublin.

GLEN JACKSON

MUM'S MARINATED CHICKEN

SERVES 4

MARINADE

2 cloves garlic, crushed
½ cup good-quality tomato sauce
¼ cup barbecue sauce
2 tablespoons sweet chilli sauce
2 tablespoons soft brown sugar
1 tablespoon mustard
1 tablespoon malt vinegar
dash Sriracha or Tabasco sauce (if
 you want heat)

CHICKEN

8 chicken pieces (such as
 drumsticks), bone in

TO SERVE

cooked rice
bread and butter
cut limes, lightly grilled on a
 chargrill (optional)

Preheat the oven to 180°C. Line a shallow roasting tray with baking paper (this helps with the washing up).

Place the marinade ingredients in a large bowl and mix well.

Add the chicken to the bowl and toss well to coat. Tip the chicken out onto the tray and spread out in a single layer, covered with marinade.

Bake for 40–45 minutes, or until cooked through, basting the chicken with the marinade twice during this time. The cooking time will depend on the size of your drumsticks—check whether they are done by cutting into the thick part of a drumstick; there shouldn't be any pink bits.

Serve the chicken with rice, mopping up the sauce with bread and butter. Squeeze lime juice over for added flavour, if desired.

GLEN JACKSON is a former rugby player turned full-time professional referee, and is widely regarded as one of the world's top officials. His career highlights include the appointment to referee the 2016 Investec Super Rugby final between the Hurricanes and Lions, as well as refereeing at the 2015 Rugby World Cup.

ROAST CHICKEN WITH LEMON & ROSEMARY

SERVES 4

2 tablespoons olive oil, plus extra for drizzling

1 red onion, finely chopped

40 g pancetta, diced

½ small lemon, well washed and finely diced (use both skin and flesh)

2–3 tablespoons rosemary leaves, finely chopped

salt and freshly ground black pepper

1 cup sourdough bread cubes

1.5 kg whole free-range chicken

25 g butter, softened

2 cloves garlic, crushed

good splash of balsamic vinegar

Preheat the oven to 200°C.

Pour the olive oil into a frying pan and place over a low heat. Add the onion and cook, stirring occasionally, until soft and just beginning to colour. Add the pancetta and cook until it begins to crisp, then add the diced lemon and half of the chopped rosemary. Cook for a further 1 minute, then season with pepper. Remove from the heat, stir through the bread cubes and allow to cool.

Using paper towels, pat the chicken dry inside and out. Mix together the softened butter, garlic and remaining chopped rosemary. Season with salt.

Gently slide your hand under the skin of the chicken to loosen it. Rub the butter mixture into the chicken, rubbing it over and under the skin.

Stuff the cavity with the cooled bread stuffing. Tie the legs together with kitchen string to keep the stuffing in, and use skewers or toothpicks to hold the wings to the chicken frame. Place the chicken in a roasting dish and drizzle over a little extra olive oil. Roast for 1 hour 15 minutes, basting from time to time by spooning the cooking juices over the chicken.

Remove the chicken from the oven and splash over a little balsamic vinegar. Carve the chicken and serve drizzled with the roasting juices. Some parsnip mash and a big bowl of steamed vegetables would be perfect with this dish.

BEN SMITH has had a spectacular rugby career since his debut for the All Blacks in 2012. He appeared in every Test when the All Blacks became the first side in the professional era to go through the season unbeaten. Ben also won a Commonwealth Games gold medal with the All Blacks Sevens team in Delhi in 2010.

Clockwise from top left: Ben Smith; Ben's masterpiece in progress; Waisake Naholo; Liam Squire.
Opposite: Waisake & Ben.

NATE'S GO-TO CHICKEN WITH BROCCOLI SLAW

SERVES 4

RAW BROCCOLI SLAW

1 head of broccoli, finely chopped
1 carrot, peeled and coarsely grated
1 green apple, cored and sliced
½ red onion, very finely sliced
½ cup toasted walnuts, roughly
   chopped
¼ cup dried cranberries (optional)
½ cup good-quality mayonnaise
2 cloves garlic, crushed
1 teaspoon runny honey
good squeeze of lemon juice
salt and freshly ground black
   pepper

KUMARA MASH

4 large orange kumara, peeled and
   cut into even-sized pieces
good knob of butter
¼ cup hot milk

CHICKEN

4 x 150 g chicken breasts, boneless
   and skinless
olive oil as needed
4 tablespoons store-bought
   chunky pesto dip

NATHAN HARRIS first joined
the All Blacks in 2014 for the
Investec Rugby Championship.
He was also a member of the New
Zealand U20s side that made the
final of the 2012 Junior World
Championship.

Preheat the oven to 190°C. Line a shallow roasting tray with baking paper.

In a large bowl, combine the broccoli, carrot, apple, red onion, walnuts and cranberries, if using. Cover and keep in the fridge.

In a small bowl, combine the mayonnaise, garlic, honey and lemon juice. Season, then cover and keep in the fridge.

Place the kumara in a large saucepan of lightly salted cold water, cover the pan and bring up to the boil. Simmer until tender, about 20 minutes. Drain and return to the heat for a few minutes, gently shaking the pan while the kumara dries off.

Mash the kumara and beat in the butter and enough milk to make a soft mash. Season with salt and pepper.

While the kumara is boiling, cook the chicken. Cut a pocket 2–3 cm deep at the thickest end of each chicken breast. Place a large frying pan over a medium-high heat. Rub the chicken breasts with a little oil and season with salt and pepper. Pan-fry until golden on both sides then place in the prepared roasting tray. Fill each pocket with the pesto dip, then roast for about 12 minutes, until cooked through.

Mix the slaw and dressing together. Serve the chicken breast on top of the kumara mash, with the slaw on the side.

TIPS

- *To toast the walnuts, preheat the oven to 180°C. Spread walnuts out on a baking tray, in a single layer, and place in the oven to toast for 5–10 minutes until lightly browned. Keep a good eye on them as they can burn very easily. Tip onto a plate to cool.*

- *If you prefer, cut the broccoli into thick slices and steam until tender.*

VEGETARIAN

DELICIOUS & NUTRITIOUS NACHOS

SERVES 4

2 firm but ripe avocados, halved, stone removed and peeled
juice of 1 lemon
sea salt
2 tablespoons cumin seeds
1 teaspoon coconut oil
400 g can black beans, drained
1 packet corn chips
2 large ripe tomatoes, diced
1 cup grated Cheddar (preferably vegan)

TO SERVE
small handful of coriander leaves

Preheat the oven grill until hot.

Cut the avocado flesh into small dice and squeeze the lemon juice over the top. Season with salt and set aside.

Heat a small, dry frying pan until quite hot, add the cumin seeds and toast for a few minutes until fragrant, shaking the pan to prevent them burning. Tip onto a plate and leave to cool, then grind using a mortar and pestle or a spice grinder.

Melt the coconut oil in a frying pan, then add the black beans and ground cumin. Cook, stirring gently, until the beans are warmed through.

Using a shallow ovenproof dish, arrange the corn chips in a deep layer. Place the warmed beans on the corn chips, covering the corn chips as much as possible.

Place the avocado in the centre of the dish in a mound. Spoon on the diced tomato. Sprinkle the cheese on top, then place the dish under the grill. Grill until the cheese has melted.

Serve topped with coriander leaves.

NEIL CUDBY captained his provincial secondary schools team at the age of 16, and was just 17 when he was injured playing for Tongariro RFC. Having pulled down a driving maul in an attempt to prevent a certain try, he was forced into an awkward position and opposition players fell on top of him, dislocating his neck. He now enjoys pursuing business interests and supporting his wife and two children in their sport. A recent highlight was coaching his daughter's U8s soccer team.

CAULIFLOWER SALAD

SERVES 4

SALAD

600 g cauliflower, cut into large
  florets, then thickly sliced
1 tablespoon extra virgin
  rapeseed or olive oil
1 teaspoon ground cumin
1 teaspoon bittersweet smoked
  paprika
salt and freshly ground pepper
2 tablespoons roughly chopped
  flat-leaf parsley or coriander
good handful of roasted
  almonds, hazelnuts or walnuts,
  roughly chopped
a few black olives, preferably with
  stones removed

DRESSING

2 tablespoons lemon juice
5 tablespoons extra virgin
  rapeseed or olive oil
1 teaspoon Dijon mustard
1 teaspoon runny honey

Preheat the oven to 190°C. Line a shallow roasting tray with baking paper.

Bring a large saucepan of lightly salted water to the boil. Add the cauliflower and blanch for 4 minutes. Drain well and return to the pan.

Add the oil, cumin and smoked paprika and gently toss the cauliflower to coat it in the mixture. Season with salt and pepper and tip the cauliflower out onto the tray, spreading it out in a single layer. Roast for 15–20 minutes, until tender.

Whisk together the dressing ingredients and season with salt and pepper.

To serve, place the cauliflower in a shallow serving bowl and sprinkle with the parsley or coriander and the nuts. Scatter over a few olives to finish. Drizzle with enough dressing to moisten nicely.

LUKE ROMANO is a rugged, no-nonsense player noted for his robust defence and ability to apply pressure to the opposition with his confident lineout jumping. His elevation to the All Blacks saw him earn 11 caps in his first season in 2012, including eight starts. Luke qualified as a builder before establishing himself as a professional rugby player.

SPINACH & ZUCCHINI MINI BAKE

SERVES 4

2 tablespoons olive oil, plus extra for greasing dishes
1 onion, finely chopped
2 cloves garlic, crushed
2 tablespoons tomato paste
400 g can chopped tomatoes in juice
pinch of sugar
salt and freshly ground black pepper
3 handfuls of baby spinach leaves
handful of basil leaves, torn if large
4 small zucchini, trimmed
250 g good-quality ricotta
¼ cup freshly grated Parmesan
1 egg
½ cup grated melting cheese, such as mozzarella or Gruyère

Preheat the oven to 180°C. Lightly oil four 1-cup-capacity ovenproof dishes.

Place the olive oil in a heavy-based saucepan and warm over a low heat. Add the onion and cook, stirring occasionally, for 5-7 minutes, until soft. Add the garlic and cook, stirring, for a further 30 seconds.

Stir in the tomato paste, then add the chopped tomatoes and season with the sugar, salt and pepper. Bring to a gentle boil, then lower heat and simmer, uncovered, until the sauce begins to thicken and is full of flavour. Remove from the heat and stir in the spinach and basil.

Heat a barbecue grill or char grill until hot. Slice the zucchini lengthwise into 5-mm slices. In batches, place the zucchini slices on the grill, and grill until dark grill lines appear and the slices soften, turning the zucchini to grill on both sides. Transfer the cooked zucchini to a plate as you go.

In a bowl, stir the ricotta, grated Parmesan and egg together. Season with salt.

To assemble, spoon the tomato sauce into the base of each dish and cover with zucchini slices. Spread the ricotta mixture on top, finishing each dish with the grated cheese.

Bake until bubbling hot and the cheese mixture is golden brown, about 20 minutes.

SIONE MOLIA's eye-catching form during his Counties Manukau side's successful National Sevens campaign saw him drafted into the national squad. He cemented his place with a strong performance on debut for the All Blacks Sevens at the Las Vegas Sevens tournament.

Clockwise from top left: Phil Booth; Keenan Alexander; Sam Cane; Damian McKenzie.
Opposite: Robbie Hewitt, Phil, Damian & Nathan Harris.

VEGAN BROCCOLI & GRAPE SALAD

SERVES 4

DRESSING

¾ cup raw cashew nuts

¼ cup water

2 tablespoons good-quality maple syrup

2 tablespoons apple cider vinegar

1 clove garlic, crushed

salt and freshly ground black pepper

SALAD

1 head broccoli, cut into florets

1 small red onion, very finely sliced

2 handfuls of seedless red grapes, cut in half if large

handful of roasted salted almonds

handful of raisins (golden raisins are good here)

Place the cashew nuts in a small bowl and pour over the water. Soak for at least 2 hours or overnight. (If you have a high-speed blender, you can soak them in hot water for 10 minutes instead.)

Drain the cashew nuts and place them in a blender or food processor with the maple syrup, vinegar and garlic. Blend until very smooth and creamy, scraping down the sides a couple of times. Season with pepper and a little salt. Place in a screw-top jar and keep in the fridge until needed.

I recommend finely chopping the broccoli and leaving it raw, but if you prefer it cooked, cut the florets into thick slices and steam until just tender, then drain and leave to cool fully.

Place the broccoli, red onion, grapes, almonds and raisins in a bowl. Drizzle over the dressing and gently toss to combine. Cover and place in the fridge for about 1 hour before serving.

PHIL BOOTH was 22 when he suffered a serious neck injury while playing rugby for Melville in Hamilton, leaving him a C5/C6 tetraplegic with no feeling at all from his shoulders down and no hand function. He has gone on to achieve amazing success in life. Phil is a husband, father, engineer, inventor and innovator, who is passionate about creating new technology for the disabled sector. He is married to Julia and they are expecting their third child.

BASIL PESTO SPAGHETTI

SERVES 4

30 g walnut pieces, lightly
  toasted
60 g basil leaves
30 g Parmesan, cut into small
  pieces, plus extra for grating
50 ml olive oil, plus extra for
  drizzling
salt and freshly ground black
  pepper
juice of ½ lemon
400 g good-quality dried
  spaghetti

Place the walnut pieces, basil leaves and Parmesan pieces into a small food processor. Pulse to combine, then leave the motor running while you drizzle the olive oil in through the feed tube until you have a thick paste. Stop the food processor a couple of times during blending and scrape down the sides with a spatula.

Season the pesto with salt and pepper and add lemon juice to taste. Transfer to a bowl and drizzle a thin layer of olive oil over the surface to prevent discolouration. Cover and keep in the fridge until needed.

Bring a large saucepan of lightly salted water to the boil. Add the spaghetti and cook until al dente (tender but still with a slight 'bite'; follow the time suggested on the packet). Drain, then stir through a generous amount of pesto.

Pile onto warmed plates and finish by grating over a little extra Parmesan before serving.

TIP

· *To toast the walnuts, preheat the oven to 180°C. Spread walnuts out on a baking tray, in a single layer, and place in the oven to toast for 5–10 minutes until lightly browned. Keep a good eye on them as they can burn very easily. Tip onto a plate to cool.*

RUBY TUI has been a regular fixture in the Black Ferns Sevens team since being discovered in the Go4Gold campaign in 2012 (a recruitment drive to introduce talented sportswomen to sevens). She was named Black Ferns Sevens Player of the Year in 2017, and off the field is a regular contributor to the SKY TV commentary booth.

Clockwise from top left: Kelly Brazier; Ruby Tui; Sarah Goss; Kelly & Sarah.
Opposite: Ruby & Sarah.

RICE, QUINOA & BEETROOT SALAD WITH GOAT'S CHEESE TOAST

SERVES 4

SALAD

1–1½ cups quinoa-rice blend (consists of red quinoa, brown and black rice; or use white quinoa on its own)
500–600 g small or baby beetroot
salt and freshly ground black pepper
1 tablespoon olive oil
½ red onion, very finely sliced
good handful of flat-leaf parsley leaves, chopped
4 good handfuls of baby spinach or rocket leaves

DRESSING

finely grated zest and juice of 1 orange
2 tablespoons apple cider vinegar
4 tablespoons olive oil

TO SERVE

4 slices sourdough bread, toasted
soft goat's cheese for spreading

Place the quinoa-rice blend in a bowl, cover with cold water and leave to soak for 30 minutes. When ready to cook, preheat the oven to 190°C.

Place the beetroot in a single layer in a roasting dish. Drizzle with oil and season with salt. Pour 250 ml cold water into the dish, then cover tightly with foil. Roast for about 45 minutes, or until the point of a small sharp knife slips easily into each beetroot.

Leave the beetroot to cool a little. While they are still warm, rub the skins off and discard the skins. Cut the beetroot into wedges.

While the beetroot is roasting, cook the quinoa-rice blend. Drain off the water, and place the grains in a heavy-based saucepan. Add 1½ cups of water for every cup of dry grains used. Bring to the boil, cover, reduce the heat to a simmer and cook for 22 minutes until the liquid has been absorbed. The rice will have a slightly chewy texture. You don't need to let it cool before using it in the salad.

In a small bowl, whisk together the dressing ingredients. Season with salt and pepper.

In a large bowl, combine the quinoa-rice blend, beetroot, red onion, parsley and spinach or rocket leaves. Drizzle over the dressing and use a fork to gently mix the ingredients—you don't need to be too fussy about this.

Serve with toasted sourdough bread, generously smeared with soft goat's cheese.

CHARLIE NGATAI is one of the Māori All Blacks' most experienced backs and a respected leader in the team. He plays Investec Super Rugby for the Chiefs and provincial rugby for Taranaki. Charlie also played one Test match for the All Blacks against Samoa in 2015. In early 2018 he signed a two-year contract with French club Lyon.

ROASTED CAPSICUM & TOMATO SALAD

SERVES 4

SALAD

2 red capsicums, core and seeds
  removed
1 yellow capsicum, core and seeds
  removed
2 pita breads, split in half
  horizontally
¾ teaspoon sumac
3–4 ripe tomatoes, cut into
  wedges
1 small red onion, very finely
  sliced
4 small radishes, cut into wedges
½ cucumber, sliced or diced
small handful of basil leaves

DRESSING

1 clove garlic, crushed
2 tablespoons lemon juice
5 tablespoons extra virgin olive oil
salt and freshly ground black
  pepper

Heat an oven grill until very hot. Place the capsicums under the grill, and grill until the skins are blackened, turning the capsicums from time to time. Transfer to a bowl, cover and let them sit and steam for at least 10 minutes.

Meanwhile, place the split pita breads under the grill, and grill for a few minutes on each side until browned and crisp. Remove and place on a wire rack. Sprinkle the pita breads with sumac.

Peel the blackened skins off the capsicums and discard. Cut the capsicums into strips and place in a serving bowl along with the tomato, red onion, radish, cucumber and basil.

Whisk the garlic, lemon juice and oil together in a small bowl. Season with salt and pepper, then drizzle over the salad.

Break the pita breads into pieces and scatter over the salad. Serve straight away.

TIP

· *Try using both red and green tomato varietals in this dish.*

WAISAKE NAHOLO made his All Blacks debut in 2015. He also represented New Zealand at U20s level and in sevens, and is a member of the Taranaki Mitre 10 Cup team and the Highlanders Super Rugby club. Waisake was part of the Rugby World Cup Sevens-winning team in 2013.

TIM BATEMAN
VEGAN RAMEN

SERVES 4

TOFU

300 g packet firm organic tofu
2 tablespoons light soy sauce
1 teaspoon cornflour

NOODLES

200 g Japanese ramen noodles
2 teaspoons sesame oil

VEGETABLES

2 teaspoons sesame oil
2 good handfuls of sliced button
  mushrooms
60 g frozen corn kernels

BROTH

1 litre mushroom stock

TO FINISH

2 spring onions, trimmed and
  finely sliced
a few drops of chilli oil
4 teaspoons white miso

Preheat the oven to 200°C. Line a shallow baking tray with baking paper.

Cut the tofu into 2.5-cm cubes, pat dry with paper towels and place in a bowl. In another bowl, stir the soy sauce into the cornflour. Pour this mixture over the tofu and toss gently to coat. Spread the tofu over the baking tray and place in the oven. Cook for 15–20 minutes, turning each tofu cube over after 10 minutes.

Bring a large saucepan of lightly salted water to the boil. Add the noodles and cook according to the packet instructions. Drain well, then add the sesame oil and toss through to prevent sticking. Set aside.

Heat the sesame oil in a frying pan over a medium-low heat, add the mushrooms and corn and cook over a low heat, stirring occasionally, until the mushrooms begin to colour, about 5 minutes.

Heat the mushroom stock in a large saucepan over a medium heat until steaming hot. Meanwhile, warm four ramen bowls.

Divide the noodles between the bowls and top with the tofu and vegetables. Divide the hot broth between the bowls and finish with the slices of spring onion and a little chilli oil. Serve each ramen bowl with a teaspoon of miso to stir through.

TIM BATEMAN is a seasoned campaigner with the Māori All Blacks and has played for them since 2008. Tim made his Investec Super Rugby debut with the Crusaders when he was just 19 years old, and his rugby career has seen him take his skills to Japan for two seasons before returning to New Zealand in 2017.

Clockwise from top left: Kieran Read; Tim Bateman & Wyatt Crockett; Cody Everson; Cody & Israel Dagg.
Opposite: Tim Bateman.

CHILLI, LIME & MANGO SALAD

SERVES 4

1 lettuce (e.g. red oak), leaves washed and dried

16 spears asparagus, trimmed and steamed, or 4 small zucchini, trimmed

1 mango, peeled and sliced

2 Lebanese cucumbers, diced

2 handfuls of cherry tomatoes, halved horizontally

1 small red onion, very finely sliced

1 red chilli, de-seeded and finely chopped

juice of 2–3 limes

salt and freshly ground black pepper

a handful of fresh coconut shavings (or use toasted dried coconut shavings)

Place the lettuce leaves in a large, shallow serving bowl. Top with the steamed asparagus spears, or with zucchini sliced lengthwise into thin strips using a vegetable peeler.

Add the mango slices, diced cucumber, cherry tomatoes and red onion.

Scatter over the red chilli, then drizzle over the lime juice. Season the salad with salt and freshly ground black pepper, top with the coconut shavings and serve.

TIP

- To toast the coconut shavings, preheat the oven to 180°C. Spread the shavings out on a baking tray, in a thin layer, and place in the oven to toast for 3 minutes. Remove from the oven, stir and form back into a thin layer, then return to the oven for another 3–4 minutes until golden brown. Keep a good eye on them as they can burn very easily. You may want to cook for a little less time for paler shavings. Tip onto a plate to cool.

On 16 March 1975, in a Tawa vs Poneke U19s pre-season game, **MUIR TEMPLETON** found himself returning to consciousness at the bottom of a ruck after a head-on charge carrying the ball had gone wrong, leaving him with a C6/7 neck injury. In the early years following his accident he was a regular at the Parafed games nationally and regionally. His working career spanned 35 years and he specialised in payroll for much of that time. These days his seven grandchildren keep him busy.

BEEF, LAMB & PORK

CODY EVERSON

PALEO BOWL

SERVES 1

1 cup pumpkin cubes (skin the pumpkin and cut into 2.5-cm cubes)

4 tablespoons melted coconut oil

salt and freshly ground black pepper

½–1 cup small cauliflower florets

¼ teaspoon ground turmeric

2 handfuls of finely shredded green cabbage

150 g sirloin steak, cut into thin strips

small handful of roasted cashew nuts

TO SERVE

1 tablespoon tahini

1 lime, cut into wedges

Preheat the oven to 200°C. Line a shallow roasting tray with baking paper.

Toss the pumpkin in 1 tablespoon of the coconut oil and season with salt and pepper. Spread out on the tray and roast for 20 minutes or until tender.

Meanwhile, toss the cauliflower florets in 1 tablespoon of the coconut oil and the turmeric. Add to the roasting pumpkin after 10 minutes and roast for the remaining time.

Place another 1 tablespoon of coconut oil in a frying pan over a medium heat. Add the cabbage and cook until the cabbage wilts. Place in a serving bowl.

Place the frying pan back over a medium-high heat. Toss the strips of steak in the remaining 1 tablespoon of coconut oil and season with salt and pepper. Place in the pan and cook quickly on each side until just seared.

Arrange the roasted pumpkin and cauliflower over the cabbage and top with the sirloin steak. Scatter over the cashew nuts and drizzle over the tahini. Serve with a wedge of lime to squeeze over.

TIPS

- *To melt the coconut oil, place it in a microwave-safe container and microwave on high for 10 seconds. Remove, stir and microwave for another 10 seconds, repeating until melted. Alternatively, place a sealed container of coconut oil in a bowl of hot water and leave until melted.*

On 11 June 2011, **CODY EVERSON** sustained a C6 ASIA B spinal cord injury while playing for Shirley Boys High. He rehabilitated at the Burwood Spinal Unit for six months. Cody now has impaired use/total loss of his upper limbs, trunk and lower limbs and has impaired motor power and sensation below the level of lesion. In 2015 Cody became a Wheel Black and has been to several international tournaments. He lives with his partner and new puppy.

KOREAN BARBECUE BEEF

SERVES 4

1 onion
1 spring onion, trimmed and
  sliced
3 cloves garlic, halved
½ pear, peeled and cut into pieces
¼–⅓ cup light soy sauce
3 tablespoons sesame oil
3 tablespoons soft brown sugar
½ teaspoon ground black pepper
500–600 g rib-eye or sirloin
  steak
1 tablespoon vegetable oil

TO SERVE

steamed rice
2–3 spring onions, trimmed and
  finely sliced
2 teaspoons toasted sesame
  seeds

Cut the onion in half. Thinly slice one half and set aside, then roughly chop the other half. Using a blender or food processor, blend the chopped onion, spring onion, garlic, pear, soy sauce, sesame oil, brown sugar and pepper together until smooth. Set aside. (This will be your marinade.)

Slice the beef as thinly as you can, placing the slices in a bowl as you go. (Lightly freezing the beef for about an hour first makes slicing easier.)

Pour the marinade over the beef, add the sliced onion and toss gently to combine. Cover and leave to marinate for 30 minutes on the bench top, or longer in the fridge.

Rub the oil over a barbecue flat-plate or a large frying pan and heat until very hot. Being careful not to overcrowd the flat-plate or pan, sear the marinated beef and onion until lightly browned all over.

To serve, divide the steamed rice among four bowls and top with the beef and onion. Sprinkle with spring onion and sesame seeds.

TIP

- *To toast the sesame seeds, heat a small, dry frying pan over a medium heat. Add the seeds and cook until they begin to colour and you can smell them toasting. Transfer to a plate straight away to prevent over-toasting.*

LIAM SQUIRE made his All Blacks Test debut in the Steinlager Series against Wales in 2016. He plays provincial rugby for the Tasman Mako, and is a member of the Highlanders Super Rugby club. Liam is part of the Ngāi Tahu iwi and debuted for the Māori All Blacks in 2013.

Clockwise from top left: Ben Smith; Waisake Naholo; Liam Squire looking at memorabilia; Waisake & Keith Jarvie.
Opposite: Liam Squire.

BUNLESS BEEF & VEG BURGERS

SERVES 4

500 g beef mince
1 onion, coarsely grated
1 scant cup grated beetroot
½ cup grated carrot
½ cup grated zucchini
5 egg whites, lightly beaten
2 tablespoons wholegrain
  mustard
3 teaspoons mild curry powder
sea salt
4 iceberg lettuce leaves
2 handfuls of baby spinach
1–2 tomatoes, sliced
1 firm but ripe avocado, halved,
  stone removed, peeled and
  sliced
1 red onion, finely sliced
1 cup grated cheese

In a bowl, place the beef mince, onion, beetroot, carrot, zucchini, egg whites, mustard and curry powder. Season with salt. Use clean hands to mix together until well combined. Shape the mixture into 8 patties, place on a tray, cover and place in the fridge to firm up for at least 15 minutes.

Preheat the oven to 180°C. Line a shallow baking tray with baking paper.

Remove the patties from the fridge and place on the lined tray. Bake for 20 minutes or until cooked through.

Serve the patties in the iceberg lettuce leaves, topped with baby spinach, tomato slices, avocado slices, red onion slices and a sprinkling of grated cheese. Eat as you would eat a wrap.

TIP
- *Brush the beef patties with a little olive oil before cooking to give extra colour.*

Generally regarded as the best openside flanker in the world, **RICHIE McCAW ONZ** captained the All Blacks for a record 110 Test matches, including both the 2011 and 2015 Rugby World Cup-winning campaigns. He also holds the record for most matches played for the All Blacks, at 149. Richie was awarded the Order of New Zealand in 2016 and is one of only 20 living New Zealanders who hold this honour. He is a patron of the Rugby Foundation.

SPAGHETTI BOLOGNESE

SERVES 4

2-3 rashers rindless streaky bacon, diced
1 onion, finely chopped
2 cloves garlic, crushed
2 anchovy fillets, drained of oil and finely chopped
1 teaspoon dried oregano
4 tablespoons mixed chopped fresh herbs, such as rosemary, sage and thyme
500 g beef mince
2 sticks celery, trimmed of strings with a vegetable peeler and sliced
1 carrot, peeled and coarsely grated
250 ml red wine
400 g can chopped tomatoes in juice
1-2 cups salt-reduced beef stock
1 tablespoon soft brown sugar (optional)
salt and freshly ground black pepper
1 tablespoon finely chopped flat-leaf parsley

TO SERVE

400 g good-quality dried spaghetti
Parmesan, for grating over

Heat a large, deep frying pan over a medium heat. Add the bacon and cook for about 2 minutes until the bacon fat begins to render down. Add the onion and cook, stirring occasionally, for a further 5 minutes. Add the garlic, anchovy fillets, dried oregano and fresh herbs and cook, stirring, for a further 1 minute. Transfer the mixture to a plate.

Add the beef mince to the hot pan and cook until the mince begins to brown, about 10 minutes. Use a wooden spoon to break up lumps of meat. Add the celery and carrot and return the bacon mixture to the pan.

Pour the red wine into the pan and allow it to bubble up. Add the tomatoes, 1 cup of the beef stock and the brown sugar, if using. Bring to a gentle boil, then simmer, uncovered, over a medium-low heat for 30-40 minutes, adding more stock if necessary and stirring occasionally to prevent it sticking. Cook until you have a thick sauce that is full of flavour. Taste and adjust the seasoning with salt and pepper, then stir through the parsley.

Meanwhile, bring a large saucepan of lightly salted water to the boil. Add the spaghetti and cook until al dente (tender but still with a slight 'bite'—follow the time suggested on the packet).

Divide the spaghetti among serving bowls, top with Bolognese sauce and grate over some Parmesan cheese just before serving.

Quick-stepping fullback **NEHE MILNER-SKUDDER** debuted for the All Blacks in 2015. He plays for provincial side Manawatū and the Hurricanes Super Rugby club. He was also part of the Māori All Blacks side who played against the British and Irish Lions in 2017.

Clockwise from top left: Tane Norton & Fiao'o Faamausili; Niall Williams; Tyla Nathan-Wong, Sir Bryan Williams & Niall; Tane & Fiao'o. Opposite: Nehe Milner-Skudder.

MEATBALLS WITH SPAGHETTI

SERVES 4

3 tablespoons olive oil

1 medium-sized onion, finely chopped

500 g good-quality beef or lamb mince

400 g can cannellini beans, drained and smashed

1 teaspoon dried oregano

1 egg

salt and freshly ground black pepper

300 ml tomato passata (or tomato pasta sauce of your choice)

300 ml chicken or vegetable stock

TO SERVE

1 cup grated tasty Cheddar

400 g good-quality dried spaghetti

1-2 tablespoons roughly chopped flat-leaf parsley

Coming from a touch rugby background, **NIALL WILLIAMS** picked up sevens in 2014 and quickly impressed, debuting for the Black Ferns Sevens only a year later. She has pace and strength and excels in defence, which has helped her command a regular starting spot.

Place 1 tablespoon of oil in a small frying pan over a low heat. Add the onion and cook, stirring occasionally, for about 5 minutes until the onion is soft. Remove from the heat and cool.

Place the mince in a large bowl with the smashed cannellini beans, oregano and egg. Season with salt and pepper and add the onion. Mix well, using clean hands, then roll into 16 meatballs. Place the meatballs on a plate as you go, cover and place in the fridge to chill for at least 30 minutes.

When you are ready to cook, heat the remaining oil in a large frying pan that has a lid. In batches, add the chilled meatballs and brown gently on all sides, transferring the browned meatballs to a clean plate. When all the meatballs are done, place them back in the frying pan and pour over the tomato passata and the stock. Mix gently to combine, then cover with the lid and cook gently for 25–30 minutes. Alternatively, place the meatballs and sauce in an ovenproof dish and cook in an oven preheated to 180°C for 25–30 minutes.

Meanwhile, bring a large saucepan of lightly salted water to the boil. Add the spaghetti and cook until al dente (tender but still with a slight 'bite'; follow the time suggested on the packet). Drain, reserving some of the cooking water.

When ready to serve, add a little of the reserved cooking water to the meatballs and their sauce, if needed. Divide the spaghetti between four warmed shallow bowls. Place the meatballs and sauce on top and sprinkle with grated cheese and parsley.

TIP

• *Add greenery by gently stirring a good handful or two of baby spinach leaves into the meatballs and sauce a couple of minutes before serving.*

SCOTCH FILLET OF BEEF WITH BRUSSELS SPROUTS

SERVES 6-8

1.5 kg whole scotch fillet of beef, at room temperature
1 tablespoon Dijon mustard
1 tablespoon chopped rosemary leaves
½ tablespoon chopped thyme leaves
oil, for rubbing
salt and freshly ground black pepper
800 g Brussels sprouts
50 g butter
2 tablespoons chopped flat-leaf parsley

TO SERVE

horseradish sauce (we love New Zealand-made Mandy's Horseradish Sauce)

Preheat the oven to 210°C.

Rub the scotch fillet with the Dijon mustard, rosemary, thyme and a little oil. Season with pepper. Roast for 1 hour for medium-rare beef. Remove from the oven and season with salt. Cover with foil and a clean tea towel and leave to rest for at least 20 minutes.

Meanwhile, place a saucepan of salted water on to boil. Trim off and discard the outer leaves of the Brussels sprouts. Cut a small cross in the base of each sprout. Place in the boiling water and cook for 5–10 minutes, depending on their size. Test the sprouts for tenderness with the point of a small sharp knife. When the sprouts are softened but still on the firm side, remove from the heat and drain well.

Melt the butter in a frying pan, add the sprouts and cook for 1–2 minutes. Season with salt and pepper and scatter with the parsley.

Slice the beef and serve with the Brussels sprouts and a small bowl of horseradish sauce on the side.

TIP
- *A large dish of creamy layered potatoes would go well with this beef.*

AKIRA IOANE stood out for the New Zealand Secondary Schools team before debuting for the All Blacks Sevens in 2014, where he helped the team achieve their 12th World Series title. Akira was also a member of the 2015 New Zealand U20s side that won the World Championship title. He was selected for the All Blacks in 2017.
RIEKO IOANE's outstanding pace and strength saw him debut for the All Blacks in 2016. The speedy outside back has also represented New Zealand in sevens and went to the Rio Olympics with the team in 2016. He was named Breakthrough Player of the Year at the World Rugby Awards in 2017.

BEEF BRISKET IN STEAMED BUNS

SERVES 8 WITH LEFTOVERS

1 tablespoon coriander seeds
1 tablespoon cumin seeds
1 tablespoon yellow mustard
  seeds
½ tablespoon whole black
  peppercorns
½ tablespoon soft brown sugar
½ tablespoon bittersweet
  smoked paprika
good pinch of cayenne pepper
1 kg beef brisket
250 ml beef stock
flaky salt

TO SERVE

¼ cup good-quality barbecue
  sauce
8 Chinese steamed buns (or
  slider buns), warmed
crunchy coleslaw (optional)

Place a small, dry frying pan over a medium heat. When hot, add the coriander seeds, cumin seeds, yellow mustard seeds and peppercorns and toast until fragrant, shaking the pan to prevent them burning—you can tell by the smell when they are ready. Immediately tip them onto a plate to cool, then lightly crush them in a spice grinder or with a mortar and pestle. Tip the ground spices into a bowl and mix with the sugar, smoked paprika and cayenne pepper.

Place the beef on a large plate and rub the spice mixture all over. Cover and place in the fridge overnight. The following day, remove the beef from the fridge and leave for a few hours to come to room temperature.

Preheat the oven to 150°C. Place the beef on a wire rack sitting inside a roasting dish. Pour in the beef stock, then cover the dish completely with foil and seal well. Cook for 5 hours, until very tender. Every hour, baste the brisket by spooning over the cooking juices. When ready, remove from the oven and sprinkle with flaky salt.

Slice off about 16 thin slices (you will not use all of the brisket) and mix with enough barbecue sauce to moisten the meat. Fill the warm buns with beef, adding some coleslaw if you like.

TIP

• *For the last hour of cooking, I like to take the beef off the rack and sit it directly in the cooking juices.*

SAM CANE has had an exceptional rugby career since making his Investec Super Rugby debut for the Chiefs in 2010. He was a member of the U20s team that won the 2011 IRB Junior World Championship, then debuted for the All Blacks in 2012 at the age of 20. Sam also helped the Chiefs to win back-to-back Investec Super Rugby titles in 2012 and 2013.

KURT BAKER

SLOW-BRAISED BEEF CHEEKS

SERVES 4

3 tablespoons standard flour
salt and freshly ground black
  pepper
600–650 g beef cheeks, trimmed
  of all silver skin
3 tablespoons olive oil
2 sticks celery, trimmed of strings
  with a vegetable peeler and
  finely diced
1 carrot, peeled and very finely
  diced
1 onion, finely diced
2 cloves garlic, crushed
3–4 strips of orange rind
2 bay leaves
250 ml red wine
250 ml beef stock
400 g can chopped tomatoes in
  juice

TO SERVE
handful of flat-leaf parsley leaves,
  finely chopped

Preheat the oven to 160°C.

In a small bowl, season the flour with salt and pepper and stir to mix.

Heat a large frying pan over a medium-high heat. Dust the beef cheeks with the seasoned flour. Add 2 tablespoons of the oil to the pan, and when hot add the beef cheeks and brown for a few minutes on each side. Transfer to a casserole dish that has a tight-fitting lid.

Reduce the heat under the pan to medium, add the remaining oil, then the celery, carrot and onion and cook, stirring occasionally, for 5–7 minutes until soft. Add the garlic, orange rind and bay leaves and cook, stirring, for a further 1 minute.

Pour in the red wine and bring to the boil, then boil gently until the wine has reduced by half. Add the beef stock and tomatoes and bring the mixture back to the boil. Season with salt and pepper. Pour the mixture over the beef cheeks in the casserole dish, then cover with a layer of baking paper and the lid and place in the oven. Cook for 3½ hours, until the beef cheeks are almost falling apart. Stir halfway through cooking and check the seasoning, adjusting if necessary.

When the meat is done, remove the dish from the oven and discard the bay leaves. Stir through the parsley.

I like to serve this with cooked pappardelle pasta and a bowl of steamed broccoli.

KURT BAKER is a senior member of the All Blacks Sevens. He was part of the gold-medal-winning Commonwealth Games team in 2010 and the World Cup-winning squad in 2013. He also played for the U20s side that won the World Championship in 2014, and has been involved in four Māori All Blacks campaigns.

KEITH'S SECRET BEEF LASAGNE

SERVES 4 HUNGRY HIGHLANDERS

2 tablespoons olive oil, plus extra for greasing the dish
1 onion, finely chopped
1 clove garlic, crushed
500 g beef mince
about 530 g your favourite tomato pasta sauce
salt and freshly ground black pepper
500 g traditional cottage cheese (or ricotta)
½ cup full-cream milk
250 g packet instant lasagne sheets (you probably won't need the whole packet)
250 g mozzarella, grated
½ cup cream
¼ cup freshly grated Parmesan

KEITH JARVIE was 28 and married with two young children when he was injured on 3 May 1986. After rehab Keith lost his job and his marriage and became very depressed, but counselling helped him come out the other side. He then studied psychology and eventually started his own counselling practice. Keith is now 60 and has four grandchildren of whom he is very proud. He is retired but still leads a full and varied life.

Preheat the oven to 180°C. Grease a medium-sized ovenproof dish with a little oil.

Heat the 2 tablespoons of oil in a large frying pan over a low heat. Add the onion and cook, stirring occasionally, for 5–7 minutes until soft. Add the garlic and cook, stirring, for a further 30 seconds.

Add the beef mince and stir with a wooden spoon, breaking up the lumps of meat as you go. Cook until the mince begins to colour, then stir in the pasta sauce. Bring to a gentle boil, then lower the heat and simmer, uncovered, until you have a luscious meat sauce, about 45 minutes. Cover the pan if you find the meat sauce is reducing too quickly. Season with salt and pepper.

In a bowl, mix the cottage cheese with the milk.

Spread 2 tablespoons of the meat sauce over the base of the dish. Top with a layer of lasagne sheets, breaking them up if necessary to fit the dish. Top with half of the remaining meat sauce. Spread over half of the cottage cheese mixture, then sprinkle with half of the grated mozzarella.

Repeat the layers once more—meat sauce, cottage cheese mixture, grated mozzarella, lasagne. Pour over the cream and sprinkle over the Parmesan.

Bake for 40 minutes, or until the lasagne is al dente (tender but still with a slight 'bite') and the top is golden. If the lasagne is browning too quickly during baking, cover the dish with foil.

WARM LAMB WITH ROAST VEGETABLE SALAD

SERVES 4

ROAST VEGETABLE SALAD

4 medium-sized orange kumara, peeled and cut into rounds
2 tablespoons olive oil
salt and freshly ground black pepper
2 large beetroot, washed and cut into eighths

DRESSING

2 tablespoons red wine vinegar
5 tablespoons extra virgin olive oil
1 teaspoon Dijon mustard
squeeze of lemon juice

LAMB

3 lamb rumps (200–230 g each), trimmed of all silver skin, at room temperature
oil, for rubbing

TO SERVE

4 handfuls of baby spinach leaves
handful of flat-leaf parsley leaves, finely chopped

KELLY BRAZIER is a stalwart of both the Black Ferns and Black Ferns Sevens teams. Her impressive rugby career includes World Cup titles in both forms of the game and an Olympic silver medal. Following the 2017 International Women's Rugby Series, Kelly was third on the Black Ferns' all-time points scorers list.

Preheat the oven to 190°C. Line a large, shallow roasting tray with baking paper.

Place the kumara in a bowl and drizzle with half the oil. Season with salt and pepper and toss to combine. Tip out onto the tray, arranging the kumara in a single layer at one end.

Add the beetroot to the bowl and drizzle with the remaining oil, toss well and tip out onto the other end of the tray. (Keeping the vegetables separate during roasting means that they retain their own colour.) Roast until tender, about 40 minutes. The beetroot may take a little longer.

Place the vinegar, oil and Dijon mustard in a small bowl and whisk together. Season with salt and pepper and a squeeze of lemon juice. Set aside.

Rub the lamb rumps with a little oil and season with pepper. Heat a frying pan over a medium-high heat, place the lamb in the pan and brown quickly on each side. Transfer the lamb to the oven—place it beside the roasting vegetables and cook for 10–12 minutes for medium-rare.

Remove the lamb from the oven, transfer to a warmed plate and season with salt. Cover with foil and a clean tea towel and leave to rest for 10 minutes.

To serve, place the kumara and beetroot in a shallow serving bowl, layering them with the spinach. Drizzle over half the dressing. Slice the lamb across the grain and arrange on top. Drizzle over the remaining dressing and sprinkle with the parsley.

TIPS

- *If the beetroot is very fresh, you don't need to peel it.*
- *Cut the vegetables the same thickness so that they roast evenly and are tender at the same time.*

WYATT CROCKETT

PULLED SLOW-COOKED LAMB SHOULDER

SERVES 8

4 cloves garlic, crushed
1 tablespoon flaky sea salt
½ tablespoon freshly ground
  black pepper
2 tablespoons sweet smoked
  paprika
1 tablespoon yellow mustard
  seeds
1½ tablespoons soft brown sugar
2 tablespoons chopped rosemary
  leaves
2–2.5 kg whole lamb shoulder
¼ cup mild mustard
½ cup white wine
½ cup water

Preheat the oven to 140–150°C.

In a small bowl, place the garlic, salt, pepper, paprika, mustard seeds, brown sugar and rosemary and stir to mix.

Place the lamb in a roasting dish and rub it with the mustard, then cover it evenly with the spice mixture. Pour the white wine and the water into the base of the dish so the liquid settles around the lamb.

Cover the dish with a large piece of baking paper and then a piece of foil, sealing it well. Slowly roast for 5 hours, basting the lamb with its juices 2–3 times during cooking, until the meat is very tender.

Use two forks to pull the lamb from the bone and shred it roughly. The boys just love this tender meat served on buttered bread rolls.

TIP

• *You can also cook the lamb in a smoker. Prepare the smoker for indirect cooking over a very low heat: 110–130°C. Add wood pieces to the charcoal. Place the lamb on the cooking grill, close the lid and cook for 8–9 hours. (If using a meat thermometer, the internal temperature should reach 93°C.)*

Since his All Blacks debut in 2009, **WYATT CROCKETT** has become one of the most experienced players in New Zealand, as well as one of international rugby's best front-row forwards. In 2017 he set (and extended) a new competition record for the most Investec Super Rugby appearances.

ROAST LEG OF LAMB

SERVES 8 WITH LEFTOVERS

LAMB

2–2.5 kg leg of lamb, at room
   temperature
50 g butter
3 cloves garlic, crushed
1 teaspoon chopped thyme
   leaves
sea salt and freshly ground black
   pepper
1–2 handfuls of thyme sprigs
2 onions, sliced
½ cup olive oil

SAUCE

1 cup beef stock
¾ cup crème fraîche or
   traditional sour cream
finely grated zest of 1 lemon
1 tablespoon wine vinegar
1 bay leaf

TO SERVE

redcurrant jelly or quince jelly
   (optional)

Preheat the oven to 160°C.

Use a sharp knife to make 4–5 shallow slits in the flesh of the lamb. In a small bowl, mix together the butter, garlic and chopped thyme. Push the butter mixture into the slits and sprinkle the lamb with salt and pepper.

Place the thyme sprigs and sliced onion in the base of a roasting dish and sit the lamb on top. Drizzle the olive oil over the top. Roast for 2¼ hours.

Transfer the lamb to a board and tip all of the roasting juices into a saucepan. Replace the lamb in the roasting dish and return it to the oven for another 30 minutes.

Remove the dish from the oven, cover it loosely with foil and a clean tea towel and leave to rest for at least 10 minutes.

To make the sauce, skim the fat off the roasting juices in the saucepan. Add the beef stock to the remaining liquid and bring to the boil. Reduce the heat to a simmer and add the crème fraîche or sour cream, lemon zest, vinegar and bay leaf. Continue simmering, uncovered, until the sauce reduces a little (it will be a thin sauce). Season with salt to counteract the acidity. Strain the sauce into a warmed jug and keep hot.

I like to serve carved slices of lamb with the sauce and steamed vegetables, including potatoes. A small dish of redcurrant jelly or quince jelly is great here, too.

Former All Blacks first five-eighth **GRANT FOX**, together with Steve Hansen and Ian Foster, is currently responsible for selecting All Blacks squads. Throughout his playing career, Grant scored 1067 points during 78 matches in the black jersey.

TIP

- *To roast a 1.5 kg boneless, rolled leg of lamb: Untie the lamb and fill the cavity with 2–3 sprigs of rosemary and a small handful of thyme leaves. Roll up again and tie securely with kitchen string. Rub half the quantity of the butter garlic mixture given above over the lamb and season with salt and pepper. Roast the lamb in a 230°C oven for 20 minutes, then reduce the heat to 200°C and roast for a further 40 minutes. This will give you lamb that is still slightly pink in the middle.*

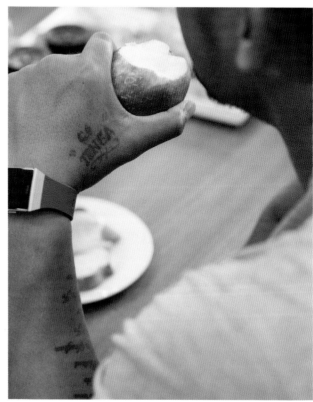

Clockwise from top left: Sonny Bill Williams & Patrick Tuipulotu; Ofa Tuungafasi; Ofa fuelling up; Ofa & Matt Duffie.
Opposite: Matt Duffie & friends.

INDIAN-STYLE LAMB SHANKS

SERVES 4

1 tablespoon vegetable oil
3 tablespoons standard flour
salt and freshly ground black
  pepper
4 lamb shanks
3 tablespoons Indian spice paste
  (I use rogan josh spice paste)
250 ml beef stock
400 g can chopped tomatoes in
  juice
6–8 shallots, peeled and halved,
  or left whole if small
8 baby carrots, trimmed and
  scrubbed

TO SERVE
handful of coriander leaves
flat-breads
natural unsweetened yoghurt

Preheat the oven to 160°C.

Place the oil in a stovetop-safe casserole dish that has a tight-fitting lid and heat over a medium-high heat. In a small bowl, season the flour and stir to mix. Dust the lamb shanks in the seasoned flour, then place in the hot oil and brown for about 5 minutes on each side.

Add the spice paste and stir to coat the lamb shanks. Cook for 1 minute. Add the beef stock and tomatoes and bring up to the boil. The liquid should just cover the lamb shanks. Season with salt. Add the shallots and carrots and stir through.

Cover the dish with its lid and place in the oven. Cook for 3 hours, or until the meat is almost falling off the bone.

Serve the lamb shanks topped with coriander leaves, with flat-breads and yoghurt on the side.

PATRICK TUIPULOTU made his debut for the All Blacks in 2014 after an impressive first campaign for the Blues during that year's Investec Super Rugby season. The high-quality lock also plays for Auckland in the Mitre 10 Cup and for Ponsonby at club level.

PORK BELLY WITH COCONUT KUMARA

SERVES 6

1.5–2 kg pork belly
1 tablespoon Sichuan peppercorns
1 teaspoon whole black peppercorns
2 tablespoons flaky salt
2 teaspoons Chinese five spice powder
2 teaspoons sugar
2 cups chicken stock
5-cm piece fresh ginger, peeled and chopped
1 red chilli, finely sliced
2 star anise

COCONUT KUMARA

3–4 medium-sized kumara, peeled and cut into even-sized pieces
2.5-cm piece of vanilla bean, split to release seeds
200 ml coconut cream
50 g butter

NICK BRIANT is one of the senior members of the New Zealand High Performance Referee squad. His experience has seen him perform at the highest level in rugby sevens, including the 2016 Rio Olympic Games, two Commonwealth Games campaigns and the HSBC Sevens World Series.

If the skin of the pork belly is not already well scored, use a sharp knife to make deep cuts diagonally across the skin, without cutting into the meat. Set aside.

Place the peppercorns in a small, dry frying pan over a medium heat and toast for a few minutes until aromatic, shaking the pan so that they toast evenly. Grind in a spice grinder or with a mortar and pestle. Place in a bowl with 1 tablespoon flaky salt, the five spice powder and the sugar. Mix together, then rub the spice mixture all over the pork belly. (At this point you can cover the pork belly and place it in the fridge overnight to marinate. Allow it to come back up to room temperature before cooking.)

Preheat the oven to 130°C. Place the pork belly, skin side up, on a wire rack sitting in a roasting dish. Rub the skin with the remaining flaky salt. Mix together the chicken stock, ginger, chilli and star anise and pour into the roasting dish. Cover the dish with foil and roast for 4–5 hours, until very tender. Remove from the oven 2–3 times during roasting and baste the pork by spooning over the roasting juices.

Turn the oven grill to high. Remove the foil and place the pork belly under the grill. Grill until the skin is golden and crackling, watching carefully to ensure it does not burn.

When the pork belly is nearly cooked, place the kumara in a saucepan with the vanilla bean, coconut cream and butter and add enough cold water to just cover the kumara. Cover with a lid and bring to a gentle boil over a medium-high heat, then reduce the heat and simmer until the kumara is tender, about 30 minutes. Drain, reserving the cooking liquid. Mash the kumara, adding the reserved liquid in small amounts until you have a soft, smooth purée.

Carve the pork belly into thick slices. Serve alongside the coconut kumara.

DESSERTS

ANTON LIENERT-BROWN

HOMEMADE VANILLA CUSTARD WITH FRESH FRUIT

SERVES 4

1 vanilla bean, split to release
  seeds
500 ml full-cream milk
6 egg yolks
2 tablespoons caster sugar, plus
  extra for sprinkling
1 teaspoon arrowroot powder
in-season fruits of your choice,
  cut into bite-sized pieces

Place the vanilla bean and milk in a heavy-based saucepan over a medium heat and bring the milk up to scalding point (just before it boils). Remove from the heat and leave for 10 minutes to allow the vanilla to infuse into the milk.

In a heatproof bowl, mix together the egg yolks, sugar and arrowroot powder. Pour the infused milk into the bowl, stirring continuously until combined.

Rinse out the saucepan, then pour the custard mixture into it. Cook over a medium-low heat, stirring continuously with a wooden spoon, until the custard thickens enough to coat the back of the spoon.

Remove the vanilla bean. Pour the custard into a jug and sprinkle the surface with a little extra caster sugar to prevent a skin forming.

Serve the vanilla custard with seasonal fruit.

TIPS

- *The arrowroot powder helps to stabilise the custard and will thicken it a little as well.*
- *If you wash and dry the vanilla bean carefully to remove all of the milk, you can use it again.*

ANTON LIENERT-BROWN was a member of the champion New Zealand U20s side in 2015, and was first called into the All Blacks for the Investec Rugby Championship in 2016. He plays Investec Super Rugby for the Chiefs. In 2016 he also helped Waikato secure the Ranfurly Shield.

SAM WHITELOCK
PAVLOVA

SERVES 6-8

4 egg whites, at room
  temperature
pinch of salt
1 cup caster sugar
2 teaspoons cornflour
1 teaspoon vinegar
½ teaspoon vanilla extract
300 ml whipped cream
sliced fresh fruit and berries
  (I love sliced strawberries and
  raspberries)
handful of freeze-dried
  raspberries

Preheat the oven to 180°C. Draw a 20-cm-diameter circle on a sheet of non-stick baking paper and place it on a baking tray, with the marked circle facing down (you should still be able to see the circle).

Using an electric mixer or an electric hand-held beater, beat the egg whites with the salt until soft peaks form when you lift the beater from the mix.

Adding one-third at a time, beat in the caster sugar, beating well after each addition, and continue beating until the meringue is stiff and glossy.

Sift the cornflour over the meringue, add the vinegar and vanilla extract and gently fold through.

Pile the meringue onto the prepared tray and shape it out to reach the edges of the marked circle (no larger). Flatten the top and smooth the sides.

Place in the oven, reduce the heat to 150°C and cook for 1¼ hours. Turn the oven off and leave the pavlova inside for about 4 hours, or overnight, to cool completely. Don't be tempted to open the oven door during this time!

Remove the pavlova from the paper and place on a serving plate. Spread the whipped cream on top and decorate with the fresh fruit. Finish by sprinkling with the freeze-dried raspberries, crushing them lightly in your hand as you sprinkle.

SAM WHITELOCK has shouldered a big load for the All Blacks, becoming their most-capped lock of all time. He made his first Test appearance in 2012, scoring two tries on debut. Sam played in every All Blacks match at the 2011 Rugby World Cup, then repeated this feat at the 2015 Rugby World Cup. He has also captained the Crusaders for two seasons, leading the team to their eighth Investec Super Rugby title in 2017.

KEENAN ALEXANDER

CLASSIC BAKED CHEESECAKE

SERVES 8

250 g digestive biscuits, crushed
115 g butter, melted
1 teaspoon ground cinnamon
450 g traditional cream cheese
1 cup caster sugar
3 eggs
1 teaspoon vanilla extract

TO SERVE

150 ml cream, whipped, plus
   extra if desired
1 green kiwifruit, peeled and cut
   into pieces
3–4 kiwiberries, halved
   horizontally
½ green apple, thinly sliced
2 Medjool dates, stones removed,
   sliced
ground cinnamon, for dusting

Preheat the oven to 150°C. Line a 20-cm round spring-form or loose-bottomed cake tin with non-stick baking paper.

Mix together the crushed biscuits, melted butter and cinnamon, and press firmly into the base of the tin. Place in the fridge until ready to use.

Beat together the cream cheese and sugar, beating until smooth. Beat in the eggs, one at a time, then beat in the vanilla extract. Remove the tin from the fridge and pour the cream cheese mixture over the biscuit base.

Bake for 40 minutes, then turn the oven off and leave the cheesecake inside to cool for at least 1 hour. Remove from the oven to cool completely, then cover and place in the fridge for at least 4 hours.

To serve, remove the cheesecake from the tin. Top with the whipped cream and decorate with the prepared fruit. Dust with a little ground cinnamon to finish. If you like, serve extra whipped cream in a bowl alongside.

TIPS

- *You can make this cheesecake the day before you need it.*
- *Change the fruit to suit what's in season or what you have in your fruit bowl.*

KEENAN ALEXANDER is the youngest member of our VIP family. A keen outdoors person with a love of fishing and hunting, he was just 17 when he was injured playing for the Thames High School 1st XV on 8 August 2016. Nearly two years down the track, Keenan is back in Thames working after a focused rehabilitation period, and plans to take up study as well. Keenan's incredible no-nonsense attitude and wry humour shine through despite what he's been through.

Clockwise from top left: Anton Lienert-Brown & Sam Cane; Anton; Keenan Alexander; Phil Booth holding the ball.
Opposite: Anton & Robbie Hewitt.

HOT CHOCOLATE PUDDING

SERVES 4

50 g butter, melted, plus extra for greasing the dish
1 cup standard flour
4 tablespoons caster sugar
2 tablespoons dark cocoa
2 teaspoons baking powder
½ cup raisins
½ cup full-cream milk
1 egg
1 teaspoon vanilla extract

TOPPING

1 well-packed cup soft brown sugar
2 tablespoons dark cocoa
1 cup boiling water

TO SERVE

whipped cream or ice cream
dark chocolate, for grating

Preheat the oven to 180°C. Lightly grease a medium-sized ovenproof dish.

Sift the flour, sugar, cocoa and baking powder into a bowl. Stir through the raisins.

In another bowl, lightly whisk together the milk, melted butter, egg and vanilla. Add the wet mix to the dry ingredients and stir to combine. Transfer the mixture to the dish and spread out evenly.

Mix together the brown sugar and cocoa, and sprinkle this over the batter. Pour the boiling water slowly over the top.

Bake for about 40 minutes, until the pudding has puffed up and is firm to the touch. Serve with whipped cream or ice cream and grate some dark chocolate over the top, if desired.

SARAH GOSS has developed into one of the leading sevens players in the world. As well as being the current Black Ferns Sevens captain, she has several accolades to her name, including world champion in 2013, Olympic silver medallist in 2016 and four-time World Series winner. Sarah was also part of the 2017 Women's Rugby World Cup-winning side.

CRÈME BRÛLÉE

MAKES 4

500 ml cream
1 vanilla bean, split to release
    seeds
5 egg yolks
2–4 tablespoons caster sugar
1 teaspoon cornflour
extra caster sugar, for dusting

Pour the cream into a heavy-based saucepan and place over a low heat. Add the vanilla bean and bring the cream to scalding point (just before it boils). Remove from the heat. Place a little water in another saucepan and put it on a medium heat to come up to a simmer.

Place the egg yolks and sugar in a heatproof bowl. Beat using a wooden spoon until the mixture is light and creamy. Sift in the cornflour and mix. Pour the cream and vanilla bean into the bowl while stirring continuously.

Place the bowl over the pan of simmering water, ensuring that the water is not touching the bowl. Stir continuously until the custard thickens—this could take 20 minutes. Don't let it come to the boil during this time or the custard will curdle.

Remove from the heat and strain the custard into a jug, then pour it into four individual heatproof ramekins or custard cups. Allow to cool, then cover the ramekins with plastic wrap and place in the fridge. It is best to leave them in the fridge overnight or for at least 8 hours.

To finish, remove the ramekins from the fridge, uncover and dust each one with a liberal dusting of caster sugar, spreading the sugar as evenly as possible over each surface. Use a blowtorch to turn the sugar to caramel.

Place the crème brûlée back in the fridge for about 30 minutes, to chill the custard again before eating.

TIPS

- *If you don't have a blowtorch, you can caramelise the sugar under a hot oven grill, watching it carefully to ensure that it does not burn.*
- *The vanilla bean can be carefully washed and dried to remove all custard and used again.*

ROBBIE HEWITT was injured in 2009 when he was 24. He is currently co-captain of the Wheel Blacks and has had many fantastic experiences travelling the world with the team. Rob works at the Waikato Rugby Union and has a tight schedule that rivals any busy professional. He loves nothing more than heading back to the family farm in Te Aroha and going to watch his old rugby club, the mighty Waihou, dominate the Thames Valley club competition.

SIR GRAHAM HENRY

APPLE AND BLACKCURRANT SPONGE

SERVES 4-6

6 cooking apples, peeled, cored and sliced
1 cup water
½ cup sugar
125 g butter, softened
½ cup caster sugar
1 egg
1 cup standard flour
2 teaspoons baking powder
about ½ cup full-cream milk
1 cup frozen blackcurrants
1 tablespoon icing sugar, for dusting

TO SERVE

vanilla custard, ice cream or whipped vanilla-flavoured cream

Preheat the oven to 190°C. Lightly grease a 4-cup-capacity ovenproof dish.

Place the sliced apple in a saucepan together with the water and sugar. Cover, place over a medium heat and gently cook until the apple is soft, about 8 minutes. Transfer the mixture to the ovenproof dish and keep hot.

Place the butter and sugar in a bowl and beat until pale and creamy. Add the egg and beat in well. Sift the flour and baking powder together and gently fold into the creamed mixture. Gently fold in enough milk to give the batter a soft consistency that drops easily from the spoon.

Swirl the frozen blackcurrants through the hot apple. Spoon the sponge mixture over the top and place the dish in the oven. Bake for 30–35 minutes, or until the sponge is golden and springs back when lightly touched in the middle.

Remove the sponge from the oven and sift the icing sugar over the top. Serve hot with vanilla custard, ice cream or whipped vanilla-flavoured cream.

SIR GRAHAM HENRY is one of the most successful coaches to have worked with the All Blacks. During his 140 matches as coach, he led the national side to victories in five Tri Nations tournaments, three Grand Slams, a series against the British and Irish Lions and one Rugby World Cup. He also received the IRB Coach of the Year Award a record five times. Sir Graham is a patron of the Rugby Foundation.

POACHED PEARS WITH ELDERFLOWER CREAM

SERVES 4

4 cups water
2 cups sugar
juice of 1 lemon
½ vanilla bean, split to release
  seeds
4 Packham pears
1–2 tablespoons elderflower
  cordial
150 ml cream, whipped
finely grated dark chocolate

Place the water in a wide, heavy-based saucepan and add the sugar. Heat gently over a low heat, stirring, until the sugar dissolves, then increase the heat to medium and bring the sugar syrup to a simmer. Add the lemon juice and vanilla bean.

Halve and peel the pears. Leave the stems on for effect, but cut out the hard core end.

Place the pears in the simmering syrup. If the pears are not fully submerged in the syrup, cover them with a piece of baking paper, pressing the paper down onto the pears. Simmer very slowly until tender, 30 minutes or even longer. This will depend on how ripe your pears are. Once tender, leave the pears to cool in the syrup.

Gently mix enough elderflower cordial into the whipped cream to flavour it to your liking.

Serve the poached pears with a little syrup, the elderflower cream and some dark chocolate grated over the top.

RYAN CROTTY's name has been etched into All Blacks folklore after his last-minute try against Ireland in 2013 kept the team's perfect season intact. He made his debut for Canterbury as a teenager and started his career in black early, representing New Zealand Schools in 2006, winning the Junior World Championship with the New Zealand U20s side in 2008 and playing for the Junior All Blacks in 2009.

BAKING

SEAN FITZPATRICK

OLD-FASHIONED CHOCOLATE SLICE

MAKES 16 PIECES

SLICE

½ cup standard flour
½ cup self-raising flour
2 tablespoons dark cocoa
½ cup brown sugar
½ cup desiccated coconut, plus
  extra for sprinkling on top
  (optional)
125 g butter, melted and cooled
1 large egg, lightly beaten

ICING

1 cup icing sugar
3 tablespoons dark cocoa
small knob of butter
boiling water as needed

Preheat the oven to 180°C. Line a 20-cm square cake tin with non-stick baking paper.

Sift both flours and the cocoa into a large bowl. Add the brown sugar and desiccated coconut, mix to combine and make a well in the centre.

Pour the melted butter and the egg into the well, then mix until all the ingredients are combined. Press the mixture into the prepared tin and bake for 15–20 minutes.

Remove from the oven and leave to cool a little before removing the slice from the tin and transferring it to a wire rack to cool completely.

Sift the icing sugar and cocoa into a bowl. Add the butter and a splash of boiling water, and mix until you get an icing with a spreadable consistency—adding small amounts of boiling water as needed.

Ice the chocolate slice with the icing, sprinkle with extra desiccated coconut, if using, and leave to set before cutting into pieces to serve.

Store in an airtight container in the fridge for up to 1 week.

SEAN FITZPATRICK is one of the most significant All Blacks of all time. He debuted in 1986, becoming captain in 1992 and leading the side for 62 matches. Sean was made an Officer of the New Zealand Order of Merit in 1997. He holds many charitable positions, and also lends his experience as a presenter on *Sky Sports* in the UK.

DANE COLES

SPONGE CAKE

SERVES 8

butter, for greasing the tins
¾ cup caster sugar, plus extra for the tins
1 tablespoon standard flour, plus extra for the tins
4 eggs, separated
1 tablespoon boiling water
1 cup cornflour
1 tablespoon standard flour
2 teaspoons baking powder

TO SERVE

3 tablespoons jam (raspberry or plum is good)
150 ml whipped cream
1 fresh fig, cut into thin wedges
2 handfuls of blueberries
pulp from 1–2 passionfruit
ground cinnamon, for dusting

Preheat the oven to 180°C. Grease two 20-cm round cake tins with butter, then line the bases with non-stick baking paper. Sprinkle a little caster sugar around the sides of each tin, followed by a little flour. Tap each tin on the bench and turn upside-down to remove excess.

In a very clean bowl, beat the egg whites with the water until stiff. Add the sugar bit by bit, beating each time until the sugar has dissolved. One at a time, beat in the egg yolks.

Measure out the cup of cornflour then remove 1 tablespoon and return it to the packet. Sift both flours and the baking powder over the egg mixture and gently fold in.

Divide the mixture between the prepared tins and place in the oven. Bake for 20–25 minutes, until golden and springy to the touch. Remove the tins from the oven and lightly drop each one on the bench to expel air and prevent shrinking. Remove the sponge cakes from their tins, placing them on a wire rack to cool.

When ready to serve, place one of the sponge cakes on a serving plate and spread it with jam. Top with the remaining sponge cake. Spread the whipped cream over the top and decorate with the fresh fruit and passionfruit pulp. Finish with a light dusting of ground cinnamon.

All Blacks hooker **DANE COLES** is a fan favourite for the Wellington provincial team and the Hurricanes Super Rugby club. He made his national debut for the New Zealand U19s in 2005, then played for the U21s in 2007 and joined the Māori All Blacks for the team's Centenary Series in 2010. His All Blacks debut came in 2012.

BANANA & PECAN MUFFINS

MAKES 12

butter, for greasing the tin
2 cups standard flour
2 teaspoons baking soda
1 teaspoon ground cinnamon or mixed spice
½ teaspoon salt
1 cup caster sugar
½ cup desiccated coconut
1 large ripe banana (or 2 small ones), mashed
1 carrot, peeled and coarsely grated
1 green apple, quartered and cored, coarsely grated
½ cup roughly chopped pecan nuts
3 eggs
1 cup sunflower oil
1 teaspoon vanilla extract

Preheat the oven to 190°C. Grease a 12-hole muffin tin lightly with butter.

Sift the flour, baking soda, cinnamon or mixed spice and salt into a large bowl. Stir in the sugar and coconut. Add the banana, carrot, apple and pecan nuts. Mix to combine.

In a separate bowl, mix together the eggs, oil and vanilla extract. Pour the egg mixture into the flour mixture and stir until just combined, being careful not to over-mix.

Spoon the batter into the prepared muffin tin, using all the mixture to fill the holes (they should be about three-quarters full). Bake for 25 minutes.

Remove the tin from the oven and leave the muffins to cool for 5 minutes before removing them from the tin.

These muffins are great served warm with butter or whipped cream and a hot cup of tea.

On 14 April 1984, **BOB SYMON** was a 20-year-old university student 'living the dream' when he broke his neck in a mistimed scrum collapse during an inter-faculty social game. It seemed to Bob that his future was over, but he was wrong—Bob is now married to Janet and has two sons, Charlie and George, a dog called Flo and a job as IT manager for ANZ. His love of community and his passion for travel and sports bring fun and excitement to each day.

Above: Bob Symon.
Opposite: Muir Templeton & Brad Shields with his baby daughter.

FRUIT CAKE

SERVES 12

225 g butter, softened
225 g caster sugar
4 large eggs
1 teaspoon vanilla extract
225 g high-grade flour
2 teaspoons baking powder
100 g ground almonds
450 g mixed dried fruit

Preheat the oven to 160°C. Line a 23-cm square cake tin with non-stick baking paper.

In a large bowl, beat the butter and sugar together until light and fluffy. Add the eggs one at a time, beating well after each addition. Beat in the vanilla.

Sift the flour and baking powder over the egg mixture, add the ground almonds and gently fold through. Add the dried fruit and gently fold through.

Spoon the mixture into the prepared tin and smooth the top. Bake for 1–1¼ hours, or until a skewer inserted into the centre of the cake comes out clean.

Remove from the oven and leave to cool in the tin. Once fully cooled, store in an airtight container. It will keep for 2 weeks.

TIP

- *If the mixture curdles when you're beating in the last egg, beat in 1–2 tablespoons of the measured flour to stabilise the mixture.*

ARDIE SAVEA burst onto the national scene in 2012 at just 18 years old, making his first provincial appearance for Wellington. The following year he debuted for the Hurricanes Super Rugby club, as well as playing for the New Zealand U20s side and joining the All Blacks on their year-end tour as a non-playing apprentice. Away from rugby he enjoys fashion, launching his own clothing range in 2017.

DAVID KIRK

CHILLI BROWNIE

SERVES 12

250 g butter, melted and cooled
2 cups caster sugar
4 eggs, lightly beaten
½ cup dark cocoa, sifted
2 teaspoons vanilla extract
2 teaspoons dried chilli flakes
2 cups dark chocolate pieces
¾ cup standard flour

Preheat the oven to 150°C. Line a Swiss roll tin (about 30 cm x 23 cm) with non-stick baking paper.

Ensure that your butter has cooled, then add the sugar, egg, cocoa, vanilla and chilli flakes and mix together.

Gently stir the chocolate pieces through the mixture. Sift the flour over the top and mix to combine, ensuring that you don't over-mix.

Pour the mixture into the prepared tin and bake for 55–60 minutes, until just firm to the touch in the middle.

Remove from the oven and leave the chilli brownie to cool in the tin. Once cool, remove it from the tin and cut it into very small pieces. Store in an airtight container for up to 1 week.

DAVID KIRK debuted for the All Blacks in 1983 and is best known for captaining the team when they won the inaugural Rugby World Cup in 1987. David also played provincial rugby for Otago and Auckland. In 1988, he was appointed a Member of the Order of the British Empire. David has had a successful business career since retiring from rugby.

GILBERT ENOKA

CHEESE SCONES

MAKES 6-8

2 rounded cups standard flour,
   plus extra for sprinkling
½ teaspoon salt
50 g cold butter, cut into small
   pieces or coarsely grated
3 teaspoons baking powder
1 cup grated tasty cheese, plus
   ½ cup for sprinkling
1 cup milk, plus extra for brushing

Preheat the oven to 220°C. Place a baking tray in the oven to heat.

Sift the flour and salt into a mixing bowl. Add the butter and rub it in with your fingertips until the mixture resembles fine breadcrumbs.

Sift in the baking powder and add 1 cup of the grated cheese, and mix in with a round-bladed table knife. Pour the milk into the bowl and mix with the knife until just combined. You want to work quickly and lightly. The scone dough should be soft and a little bit sticky.

Tip the dough out onto a lightly floured work surface and shape the scones. You can pat the dough into a round and cut this into large triangles, or pat the dough into a rectangle and cut this into squares. The scone dough should be at least 2.5-cm thick before you cut it.

Remove the hot tray from the oven and sprinkle it with a little flour. Place the scones on the tray, keeping the pieces close together, then brush the tops with a little milk and sprinkle with the extra cheese.

Bake for 12–15 minutes, until the scones are well risen and a deep golden-brown colour. Serve warm with butter.

TIPS
· *The standard flour and baking powder can be replaced with self-raising flour.*
· *To introduce a touch of heat, add some black pepper or a good pinch of cayenne pepper along with the baking powder.*

A former New Zealand volleyball representative, **GILBERT ENOKA** has worked with the All Blacks in the area of sports psychology and mental skills since 2000. In his role as Manager—Leadership, he is involved with many aspects of the team's off-field development.

NZ RUGBY STARS COOKBOOK

INDEX

First published in 2018

Text © NZ Rugby Foundation, 2018
Photography © Tamara West and Kieran Scott, 2018

Allen & Unwin
Level 3, 228 Queen Street
Auckland 1010, New Zealand
Phone: (64 9) 377 3800
Email: info@allenandunwin.com
Web: www.allenandunwin.co.nz

83 Alexander Street
Crows Nest NSW 2065, Australia
Phone: (61 2) 8425 0100

A catalogue record for this book is available from
the National Library of New Zealand.

ISBN 978 1 76063 355 4

Design by Kate Barraclough
Set in Madera
Printed and bound in China by
Hang Tai Printing Company Limited
10 9 8 7 6 5 4 3 2 1